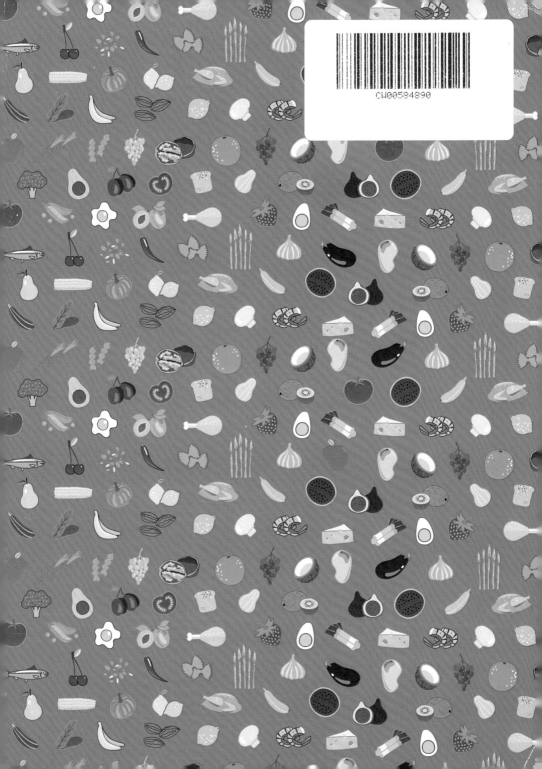

Published by Goldcrest Books
www.goldcrestbooks.com
publish@goldcrestbooks.com

ISBN: 978-1-911505-32-7

How Food
Shapes Your Child

Louise Mercieca

Meet the Team!

Captain Red Pepper Pants - he thinks eating veg is super cool!

Inspector Banana - he is on the lookout for where veg may be hiding and making sure that you are eating it

Dr Bertha Carrot - the clever one! She knows all about why food is good for you and what you should eat to be big, strong, healthy and clever!

Corporal Courgette - you don't want to make him cross by not eating your veg, he especially likes all things green!

Tammy Tomato - she loves all things with red, yellow and orange veg in as she knows these are super healthy!

Contents

The making of this book

For some time, lurking in the back of my mind, I had the idea to write a '*cook book*'. In fact, I had even started a few, but I never found the time or enthusiasm to bring them to completion.

This all changed when, as part of my Continuing Professional Development, I did a course all about how nutrition impacts on children's developing brains. Whilst studying this, and some new research and scientific studies, my passion for my book was reignited - but this time the emphasis was to be on children.

Research for the book, a snapshot of some of the many documents I have been ploughing through

So much of my nutrition work has been on preventative health, how nutrition can *sometimes* replace the need for medication and how nutrition can both heal and harm us. Suddenly, in a moment of clarity, I realised that the best form of preventative health is via our children. They are of course, the future generation and, as you will see in this book, we leave an imprint via

Even batman needs to go food shopping

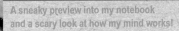

epigenetics when we have children. We have also seen that this young generation is quite unhealthy! There are increases in many lifestyle diseases, the biggest being obesity and type 2 diabetes. These are the two biggest areas of study in terms of nutritional epigenetics, and they are things that we can influence through changes to our diet.

My biggest inspiration of course, was my own little boy, aged 4 at the time of writing this book. Whilst shopping for him I realised just how difficult it can be to select healthy choices amongst a marketplace saturated with cheaper, convenient but unfortunately less healthy choices.

Picking pumpkins

I will discuss the impact diet has on our children throughout this book, but the main message I have is that YOU **can** take control. Despite moaning (whilst doing my own supermarket shop) that the choices available lean towards the unhealthy, unfortunately I don't see that changing. The food industry has a lot of power and influence. So, it is down to us to ensure that we know what is in the food we are giving our children and the impact (good and bad) that it can have on them.

The other big point I hope comes across in this book is how to make food fun and engage children. Even tiny tots can be involved in shopping, cooking, picking recipes, learning and understanding where food comes from etc.

Helping out in the Design Studio

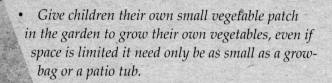

- Give children their own small vegetable patch in the garden to grow their own vegetables, even if space is limited it need only be as small as a grow-bag or a patio tub.

- Take children to farm shops to buy fruit, veg and meat, sometimes this can be a cheaper option and it certainly makes shopping more fun.

- "Pick your own" - when things are in season it's lovely to be able to involve children in picking fruits and veg.

- Invest in a small supermarket trolley so that toddlers and small children can take responsibility for some elements of their shopping, rather than spend the time bored and whinging in the supermarket. (I suggest investing in your own to take with you each time, as very few shops provide these and when they do they are few in number and very popular).

Shopping

Picking berries

- Encourage them to look at pictures in recipe books and talk to them about the photos.

3

Introduction to nutrition & health

There's lots of information out there telling us what we should and shouldn't eat, but when it comes to children it isn't that complicated, right? They move around a lot (or they should!) so surely what they eat is burnt off, as kids have a high metabolism, right?

4

This is what people have thought for a long time. However, we are now currently seeing a global health epidemic of obesity. When this relates to children, of course we can just brush it off as puppy fat, right?

Unfortunately, not!

Obesity in childhood used to be thought of as an aesthetic issue, but emerging evidence is that very young children are displaying signs that excess weight is having an adverse effect on their health. According to the Early Bird Study[1], metabolic markers for high cholesterol, abnormal glucose metabolism and blood pressure were present at the age of 9.

There are many frightening statistics around the effects of obesity and poor diet in children, here are just a few.

1. In the UK a quarter of children aged 2 to 10 are overweight or obese[2]

2. 1 in 4 five-year olds have tooth decay in their milk teeth[3]

3. In the UK a quarter of children aged 2 to 10 are overweight or obese[4]

4. It is well documented that obese youth are more at risk of a variety of health conditions; [5]

- Insulin resistance

- Type 2 diabetes

1. Tackling obesity through the healthy child programme - A framework for action, NHS/University of Leeds

2. Public Health England - Health matters - child dental health, June 2017

3. Public Health England - Childhood obesity - facts about childhood obesity

4. Public Health England - Childhood obesity - facts about childhood obesity

- Heart disease

- Arthritis

- High blood pressure, high cholesterol

- Joint and breathing issues

- Increased risk of certain cancer diagnosis

Believe me there are many more but this book isn't about that, well not just that. Of course, we can see we have a global health problem around obesity. Obesity is also not something to just shake off, it is a real medical condition.

What is the answer? That is a very big question! The first thing is to look at lifestyle. Of course, nutrition plays a hugely important role in this, and that is what I hope to achieve with this book - bringing to life the types of food that our children crave (not in the sugary craving, but what their body actually craves) to grow, develop and advance through life. It certainly isn't about calories in and energy used; whilst that is a factor it isn't everything.

Obesity isn't the only issue with the type of foods now abundantly available - children can be overweight, obese, a healthy weight or underweight, but also be malnourished. This isn't a term we hear too often in the western world as typically we associate being malnourished with starvation, but sadly this isn't the case. Diets rich in processed foods, sugar and lacking in naturally occurring micronutrients will leave children depleted. Children can easily meet their DCN (daily calorie needs) but depending on what makes up these calories, they could easily be malnourished.

There is another huge counter argument of "my child isn't fat, therefore high-fat, high-sugar foods won't harm them as they burn it off".

5. Dr Kate Northstone, Department of Social Medicine, University of Bristol – Are dietary patterns in childhood associated with IQ.

Children have under developed detoxification systems, meaning that processed foods, high-fat, high-sugar, high salt foods all place an additional burden on their system, it is not easier for them to burn it off.

Children are also growing and developing at a very fast pace! In fact, the human brain doesn't stop growing until the age of 21, so this brings me to the real issue of this book! How the food we eat as babies and children shapes our developing brain, impacts on IQ, performance at school, reading, writing, memory, behaviour and sleep.

Research shows that there is a strong association between poor eating habits, poor behaviour and poor academic performance.[6] In this book I will show you what foods aid development (and in turn will combat some of the obesity problems as we avoid the foods which fuel obesity). There is a lot of research into how consuming a high sugar diet adversely affects intellectual development, imagine the effects of blood sugar highs and lows on concentration and focus - but more on that later!

I will show ways to have fun with food, making cooking and eating an experience for the whole family to enjoy. Many people see certain foods as treats, but when you consider that some of the ingredients may be harmful (trans fats, salt and sugar) are they really a treat, even an occasional one? I touch a little bit on 'food and reward' later in this book. There are many neural pathways in place linking food with reward, these pathways become habitual and can stay with children into adulthood, meaning as adults they will continue to crave those 'treats'. This can form the basis for emotional eating as adults.

Childhood obesity – what's the issue?

Earlier I touched on the issue of childhood obesity. For me, putting this section of the book together was the most troublesome; it's hard to strike up a conversation on this subject without it potentially turning into a disagreement.

The problem is there's a whole load of contradictory information about the health of our children and often, the only issue that appears to be addressed is that of obesity. I agree that we have a problem with childhood obesity. I can see there is an epigenetic link (genetic influences), so the problem is getting worse with each generation. Obesity causes many unpleasant and serious co-morbidities - and, as I said in the introduction, this isn't just an aesthetic issue. Obesity costs the NHS around £5.1 billion each year, with that figure set to rise. So, why just focus on obesity and how is obesity being calculated?

Health, not weight

When I work with adults on nutrition, I generally tell them to throw away their scales. Instead, I rely on body composition analysis as it is a far superior measure of health than what the scales say.

When identifying childhood weight and obesity, the most common measuring tool used is the BMI or Body Mass Indicator - however, this is problematic. I know from personal experience that you can be lean with low body fat but heavy and, therefore, overweight according to the BMI scale. In fact, some professional athletes would have an obese BMI reading, yet have less than 10% body fat.

Here in lies the problem; when statistics about childhood weight and obesity are published, they include the heavier children who don't necessarily have a high percentage of body fat. Statistics exclude lighter children who sit comfortably in the healthy weight category. However, lighter children may consume a diet rich in sugar, fats and processed foods, resulting in a higher percentage of body fat and, therefore, are likely to be at risk of underlying health conditions.

There are, of course, some genuinely overweight and obese children amongst the statistics. One only has to look around any school playground to see this, but what about the real underlying health issues?

For me there are two issues: genuine weight and obesity issues, and secondary malnourishment.

Weight and obesity

I need to say something now that might touch a nerve - some children are overweight, and some children are obese. As I mentioned before, this is not just an aesthetic issue - children do not necessarily 'grow into themselves', 'grow out of it' or 'burn it off'. If your child is carrying excess fat, it is unhealthy and it is likely to affect their relationship with food as adults. It can also potentially imprint on their epigenome (chemical compounds and proteins that attach to their DNA, turning genes on or off), which results in their eating habits and weight issues being passed on to their children.

I hate to say this, but you can influence your child's weight through what they are given to eat, but please don't let this become an issue. I have seen some horror stories of young children being sent to slimming clubs - I do not advocate this approach; in fact, if there is one industry I dislike, it is the diet industry!

Don't obsess about weight!

Obsessing about calories or focusing too much on the scales, can be extremely damaging to self-esteem and creates a bad relationship with food, often for life. Children are very impressionable. Remember, parental modelling plays a big role in what your child eats. If sweets, cakes, biscuits, puddings, fast-food etc. are the norm for the adults, they will become the norm for the child too.

Food is nourishment not numerical. The number of calories does not by any means determine the nutritional value of food. Unfortunately, the calorie counting approach is still advocated by an NHS initiative based around making changes, with a focus on snacks being 100 calories or less, seemingly regardless of whether those calories are nutritious or not.

If your child does have weight to lose, do not make an issue of it or single them out. A better approach would be for the whole family to make changes, without the child knowing it's for them.

None of the recipes in the book are calorie counted, but with the right portion control, my meal ideas will fill your children up with the right balance of nutrients for their needs.

Children do need to be active. I'm not talking about structured exercise or anything that costs a lot of money - but simply walking, playing in a field with a ball, or going to the park and climbing on equipment are all great activities for children. Playing outdoors is also good for children (and adults) as exposure to vitamin D helps to lift mood and ease any potential anxieties.

There are many factors which influence weight gain and obesity; this applies to adults and children alike.

Sugar addiction

As mentioned above, sugar is very addictive. Reducing sugar in everyone's diet is essential and there are many reasons for this (enough to write a whole book). In terms of weight and health, sugar is the leading cause of obesity. Obesity is the second biggest preventable cause of cancer (second only to smoking) - here's why:

Sugar fuels fluctuating blood sugar levels, which can lead to metabolic conditions

Sugar promotes bad bacteria in the gut, which suppress the good bacteria thus weakening overall immunity and potentially causing inflammation

Sugar causes imbalances to mood, disturbs sleep patterns and confuses the body's response to feeling full (thus causing over-eating)

Trans-fat and processed foods

You will see in the table of nutrients section there are many fats which are essential to our diet. Some of these are actually called essential fatty acids, which are the only fats that we need in our diet. However, due to processed foods and fast-foods, many people including children eat far too many of the bad fats. Like sugar, these fats offer zero nutritional benefit yet actually cause quite a lot of harm in the body. The biggest culprit among the bad fats are known as trans fats.

Trans fats, e.g. margarine, are very popular in processed foods, as they're cheap and preserve the shelf life of products. Trans fats are artificial fats created using an industrial process known as 'partial hydrogenation'; turning a liquid (potentially once a healthy fat) into a semi solid fat by heating this up with hydrogen atoms.

Most processed foods will contain trans fats, and these are particularly common in:

Biscuits and cakes

Pies and pastries

Chips

Anything containing margarine

Reheated oils and fats (very common)

The consumption of trans fats has several health implications:

Trans fats have an adverse effect on blood lipids, increasing the risk of coronary heart disease (CHD). According to the British Heart Foundation, trans fats appear to increase the risk of CHD more than any other macronutrient.

Trans fats increase LDL – low density lipoproteins or bad cholesterol. Don't assume this only applies to adults. In the introduction, I mentioned the Early Bird study which reveals that metabolic markers for high cholesterol are present as young as age 9!

Trans fats are not a good source of energy. As they are artificial, the body is unable to utilise trans fats as energy, so they tend to sit around the body in fat tissues (see blood lipids and cholesterol link). Trans fats also become adipose or fat tissue under the skin (also known as subcutaneous fat) or, more alarmingly, visceral fat; this is the fat stored around the organs in the abdominal area. Remember, visceral fat is the fat you can't always see.

Trans fats hinder the role of Omega 3 and Omega 6. Therefore, eating trans fats can cause an indirect deficiency of essential fatty acids.

Deficiencies in these good fats have been linked to increased risk of cancer, heart disease, behavioural problems, depression, cognitive decline and chronic inflammation. Not a happy list!

Artificial ingredients in processed food have an adverse effect on your good gut bacteria. Children, like adults, need a healthy and diverse gut microbiome to protect them, and to ensure that they get energy and nutrients from food.

So, hopefully you will see that foods responsible for fuelling weight gain and obesity are unhealthy even in those of a healthy weight or underweight. Likewise, it would be unhealthy for underweight people to 'fatten up' with treats, thinking they can afford to because they are not visibly fat. The way to lose weight is not to restrict food or obsess about counting calories.

Malnourishment

According to the Global Nutrition report 2016, 44% of countries were experiencing under-nutrition and obesity within the same populations. The report suggests that hundreds of millions of people are malnourished because they are overweight, as well as having too much sugar, salt or cholesterol in their blood.

Within the report, one statement said the study "redefined what the world thinks of as being malnourished". Malnutrition literally means bad nutrition - that's anyone who isn't adequately nourished, not people who are actually starving.

How can this be happening to our children?

This is because…

There are a lot of empty calories around – even the NHS campaign I mentioned above, which promotes 100 kcal snacks and includes snacks containing empty calories.

Foods containing trans fats, salt and sugar are addictive, once you have the taste for them you want more.

Foods containing trans fats, salt and sugar are not filling, so you tend to eat larger quantities.

Processed foods are practically devoid of micro nutrients, vitamins, minerals, antioxidants, phytochemicals and helpful bacteria.

Artificial ingredients in food damage gut bacteria hindering micronutrient absorption

Sugar fuels bad bacteria in the gut

Trans fats hinder the absorption of essential fatty acids

There are many other reasons, but my main purpose for including all of this information is to try to encourage healthier choices for life from a very young age. Nature has provided all of the foods that we need to thrive, be healthy, evolve generationally as we did for hundreds of thousands of years. In the past 50 years, with the increase in food convenience and the addition of more sugars, trans fats and artificial ingredients, we have seen a worrying decline in health, an increase in obesity, more behavioural problems, more stress and anxiety.

For me, there is an obvious link, but I have to stress clearly that this is my own opinion – I will leave it up to you to make your own judgement.

The aim of this book is to provide health information, primarily relating to children's health, but to also provide recipes using real food for maximum nutritional gains.

Medical disclaimer

This book is not designed to replace any medical advice; I am not qualified as a doctor and I do not hold every single nutritional qualification. Through my six years of experience, I can see the many ways in which nutrition impacts on health and happiness.

Sugar

For those who know me through my nutrition or personal training work, they will know that I couldn't write a book on nutrition without paying particular attention to sugar!

I have been on a bit of an anti-sugar crusade for some time, particularly when it comes to children.

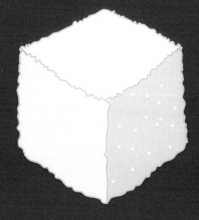

Despite many interventions, restrictions and tightening of regulations around the advertising of high sugar/high fat foods to children, there are still lots of foods aimed at children that have disproportionately high percentages of sugar for a child's needs. In fact, when it comes to sugar 'needs' there is no guideline amount for under 4's, yet many foods consumed by under 4's are high in added sugars.[1]

Foods that sneak in a lot of sugar

Yogurts

Cereals

Drinks

Jars of sauces

Sugar is a genuine addiction - studies have shown sugar to be more addictive than the class A-drug Cocaine. It is of little surprise then that once you have something sweet you want more and more of it![2]

Please don't assume that a low sugar/diet version will be a better option as these often are full of artificial sweeteners. Personally, I feel there is no place for these in a child's diet (nor adults for that matter!).

1. Public Health England – Sugar reduction – the evidence for action Oct 15

2. Institute of Health and Biomedical Innovation at Queensland University of Technology (QUT)

3. World Health Organisation – Guideline – Sugars intake for adults and children

Children like sweet things so what's the problem? As I mentioned in the introduction children have under developed detoxification systems so eating high sugar, high salt and high fat products places an unnecessary additional burden on them. There are zero nutritional benefits to many sweet treats, meaning calories are consumed without any vitamins, minerals, fibre or any notable nutritional intake. This intake of empty calories leads not only to obesity but to children and adults alike being malnourished.

The World Health Organisation has expressed concern over the high-level consumption of free sugars and how this potentially contributes to risk of death from NCD (Non-communicable diseases). Obesity is an independent risk factor for NCD's.[3]

As I mentioned in the intro, obesity is not the only risk factor amongst children. Slimmer children consuming too much sugar will potentially be at risk of the same health issues that sugar causes.

> Studies have shown that children with a daily consumption of fast-food show poorer academic achievement and slower acquisition of cognitive skills[4]

> Nutritional biochemistry shows how a child's body and brain are adversely influenced by trans fats and sugar[5]

> Childhood nutrition directly impacts on brain development affecting cognitive and educational performance[6]

In the UK a quarter of children aged 2 to 10 are overweight or obese[7]

Sugar intakes across all population groups are above the recommended guidelines[8]

Food consumption has changed dramatically in the last 30/40 years. Food is much more readily available, heavily marketed and cheaper, a bad combination for over consumption.

Consider also, the epigenetic link here, there is a growing body of research linking environmental factors such as nutritional traits acquired by parents being passed on to their children before the child is born. Studies have shown that unhealthy feeding behaviours of biological parents has a negative impact on the child, because the sperm and eggs

4. Health Science Academy – Effects of blood sugar imbalance

5. Health Science Academy – Nutrition for mood and behaviour

6. Health Science Academy – Dr David Benton PhD and Professor or phycology at Swansea University.

7. Public Health England – Childhood obesity – facts about childhood obesity

8. Public Health England – Sugar reduction – the evidence for action

9. Epigenetics – being
overweight adds distinct
epigenetic marks to DNA /
Epigenetics – could turn
on obesity switch

contained heritable epigenetic information. Studies particularly focus on obesity and type 2 diabetes as both conditions have risen significantly in the last 40 years and continue to do so.[9]

There are many initiatives in place such as the SACN (Scientific Advisory Commission on Nutrition) making recommendations to government on sugar reductions, mainly that free sugars should not exceed 5% of total dietary energy. In this book I have included many sweet recipes but not once used added white/brown/demerara sugar to sweeten. For children who are at weaning stage any foods containing added sugar should be avoided otherwise a sweet palate develops and this is hard to reverse!

Gut Microbiome

Just as I couldn't write a book about nutrition without mentioning sugar, I also had to include a section on the importance of our gut microbiome, as this is one of my favourite nutrition topics!

The human body is covered in different types of bacteria which are crucial for our health, and they all have a unique role to play and place to live on, and in our bodies; but, by far the most influential to our overall health, is the collection known as the gut microbiome, unsurprisingly this is located in our gut.

Children and adults need to have a healthy gut microbiome to support many everyday functions, such as blood sugar regulation, sleep, mood and bowel movements. But our gut microbiome is also crucial in protecting us, as the gut accounts for most of our immune system.

Our gut is very clever, it may sound strange but we do have a brain in our gut! Of course, this looks nothing like our actual brain, but the enteric nervous system is made up of a thin layer of brain located within the intestines. The enteric nervous system is host to 100 million neurons, making the gut/brain connection a crucial one for overall health.

The microbiome is (or should be) a rich diversity of life, and as with many elements of the body there are 'foods that help' and 'foods that harm' this fascinating and important aspect of our body.

This is a very simplistic take on a more complicated subject; when I do 1:1 consultations and group talks on gut health I do cover this is in a lot more detail, but in terms of trying to keep your children's gut health in check, it's probably worth checking this table as a quick guide for what to include and avoid.

Friendly foods for the gut microbiome	Why They Help
Prebiotics	Live bacteria – easiest to eat in yogurt (certainly not fruit flavoured or low-fat varieties) A particularly helpful form of plant fibre which the body can't digest, but eating prebiotics encourages good bacteria to grow. The best-known prebiotic is Inulin; this is found in onions, leek, garlic, Jerusalem artichoke and asparagus. Another form of prebiotic is beta-glucan which also aids the growth of good bacteria and lowers cholesterol levels in the blood. This can be found in oats and barley. Finally, flaxseeds which are so small they can be added into yogurts, porridge, cakes and biscuits for children (see sugar free recipes) yet they feed your microbiome and in a small way boost Omega 3 intake.
Naturally Colourful Foods (phytochemicals)	Eating a naturally occurring rainbow is beneficial in many ways, but, in relation to gut health, blue/black/purple foods such as aubergines, blueberries, blackberries, and red cabbage are all rich in anthocyanins, which encourage the growth of good bacteria such as Bifidobacterium.
Fermented Foods	Probably the easiest way to get children to have this is the drink 'Kefir'; a fermented milk drink and now available naturally flavoured – it is no use if it has added sugars or sweeteners.
Fibre	Eating fibre helps to add bulk to stools and generally is a good digestion aid. A particularly helpful element in terms of gut health is that eating fibre will help your good bacteria to produce butyrate. Butyrate helps control the growth of the cells lining the gut and is an important energy source for these cells.
Oily Fish (Omega 3 rich)	Eating foods rich in omega 3 such as oily fish is shown to increase butyrate* production. *Butyrate - an anti-inflammatory fat, beneficial for your gut.

Unfriendly foods for the gut microbiome	Why They Harm
Sugar and Trans fats	Sugar and bad fats encourage the unhealthy bad bacteria to grow, whilst at the same time suppressing the good bacteria. This is known as dysbiosis (bacterial imbalance). There is some evidence that eating a diet rich in refined sugars and trans fats will also cause constipation and bloating.
Artificial Sweeteners	Studies have shown these to lessen the good bacteria linked with slimness Akkermansia, and increase the bacteria associated with obesity and diabetes.
Processed Foods	Causes a loss of diversity to gut health – a loss of diversity here is a trigger for ill health.
Antibiotics	Yes, sometimes we all need them but repeated doses, particularly in early years, can increase the risk of Type 2 diabetes and obesity. Antibiotics eliminates both good and bad gut bacteria. If having to take/give antibiotics, try giving live yogurt or Kefir to boost probiotics and therefore the good gut bacteria.

The complex and fascinating world of the gut microbiome is one that I could carry on talking about for several pages but, for now, I hope that this table helps you to at least start to have gut health in your mind when making choices about foods to eat, and indeed those to avoid.

How to help fussy eaters

Often children will suddenly develop a new eating habit or decide they no longer like something they had happily eaten previously. The good news is that "picky eating/being unwilling to try new foods" (or to call it by its technical name, neophobia) is relatively common and children usually outgrow it. It can be frustrating while you go through this stage though, and a worry about whether they are getting all the nutrients that they need.

This actually all starts in the third trimester of pregnancy - the effect of taste is so powerful that what the mother eats at this stage in pregnancy can influence the child's food preferences once they are born. The same can be said for the mother's diet when she is breastfeeding, if the mother has a healthy varied diet the child will tend to be less picky and more willing to try new foods.

All that said, sometimes children defy all scientific logic and become fussy eaters or develop neophobia regardless of how healthy a start they had!

Children love to be recognised, praised and rewarded - I find a good way is with a reward chart. This chart does not reward with food, i.e. "you can have chocolate if you eat broccoli" as that makes food rewards an expectation and encourages inappropriate behavioural patterns and experiences in the hippocampus - neural pathways in the brain then associates and expects this reward each time.

Opposite is a sample of a reward chart to be used at home. I've designed it so that you can photocopy it easily, or it's available as a free download from my web-site. There are a couple of blank sections for you to customise it too. You can use incentives such as 10 stars = £1.00 or 20 stars = a new comic. Anything but food!

	Mon	Tues	Weds	Thurs	Fri	Sat	Sun	Total Stars for week
Tried a new food								
Didn't make a fuss at the table								
Had good table manners								
Didn't ask for sweets/chocolate								
Drank plenty of water								
Ate Breakfast								

Young children do display a preference for sweet flavours. In evolutionary terms this is because many bitter compounds in nature are toxic, so this could be a protective mechanism? The problem is that the more you feed this, the more the palate develops to expect sweet flavours as the norm, and once that happens it is then difficult to wean them back off them. Some helpful examples:

Keep to water rather than squash – squash contains little or no nutrients yet contains sugar or artificial sweeteners.

Yogurts and cereals aimed at children are often loaded with sugar, stick to natural or Greek yogurt blended with fruit, and a good cereal choice is porridge.

Children like cakes and biscuits but the volume of sugar, salt and trans-fats in shop-bought cakes can be harmful to them, - remember that children's detoxification systems are not fully developed.

Check out the baking section for naturally sweet options.

Building
a child's brain

The table shows at a glance, how certain foods can impact on brain activity.

Remember for each nutrient that does a good job there's a high sugar/fat item which will undo it!

From conception the developing baby will take it's nutrients from the mother, 50% of these nutrients go into feeding their brain growth - it's really important for Mum to eat a healthy and varied diet or the baby will 'steal' what nutrients it needs leaving Mum feeling depleted.

Main Brain Areas

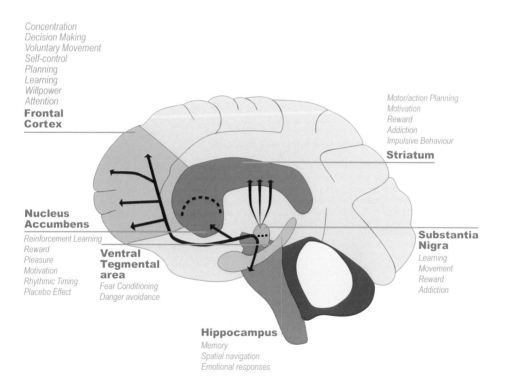

Concentration
Decision Making
Voluntary Movement
Self-control
Planning
Learning
Willpower
Attention
**Frontal
Cortex**

Motor/action Planning
Motivation
Reward
Addiction
Impulsive Behaviour
Striatum

**Nucleus
Accumbens**
Reinforcement Learning
Reward
Pleasure
Motivation
Rhythmic Timing
Placebo Effect

**Ventral
Tegmental
area**
Fear Conditioning
Danger avoidance

**Substantia
Nigra**
Learning
Movement
Reward
Addiction

Hippocampus
Memory
Spatial navigation
Emotional responses

Building a Child's Brain			
The brain is made up of 60% water and there should be 40% FAT			
Nutrients needed	**Role in Body**	**Deficiency Impact**	**Foods to include**
Fatty Acids: AA DHA EPA DGLA	These 4 fats make up 40% of the brain, crucially important for intelligence mood and behaviour. The frontal lobe of the brain should be rich in DHA helping to problem solve, focus attention and plan	Negative impact on mood IQ behaviour. During pregnancy the baby will 'steal' these so the mothers brain if deficient will get smaller! (technically known as baby-brain!)	Oily fish (salmon) rich in EPA and DHA Egg yolks Fat from dairy products
Omega 3 ALA (Alpha-linolenic acid) Essential Fatty Acid (EFA)	Involved in brain growth and development. Needed to make eicosanoids – these help to keep inflammation down in the body	Systematic inflammation is linked to many chronic diseases including; heart disease, arthritis, diabetes and certain cancers.	Oily fish, mackerel, salmon, fresh tuna, sardines, fish oil. Egg yolks (Omega 3 enriched) Flax seeds chai seeds. Seaweed or more likely a spirulina supplement
Omega 6 LA (linolenic acid) EFA	Also used to make eicosanoids. Enable cell communications Healthy skin. DNA repair and muscle growth.	Omega 6 intake in western diets generally is very high so deficiencies are unlikely.	Sunflower seeds, walnuts, pine nuts, hemp seeds, pecans, brazil nuts, sesame seeds, avocado, almonds
Phospholipids	Provide structure and protection to cells which help cellular communications. Carriers of Omega 3 fatty acids. May improve learning abilities	May struggle with concentration and attention. May show signs of difficulty comprehending tasks and grasping new concepts.	Egg yolk, oily fish, tofu, soya beans, wheat germ, nuts and seeds, milk, organ meats, lecithin granules supplement
To enable the body to properly utilise these fatty acids it needs additional nutrients; Vitamins B3, B6, E and C along with Zinc, Magnesium and Manganese.			

Helping a child to concentrate, learn and remember

Nutrients needed	Role in Body	Deficiency Impact	Foods to include
Zinc	Many different enzymes need Zinc including; Immune system function Building polyunsaturated fatty acids which are essential for brain formation and function	Reduced growth/ development, impaired immunity, low memory, impaired motor skills. When coupled with low serotonin this deficiency can increase violence, depression and anxiety.	Meat, fish (oysters are the highest in zinc but probably not the average choice for children!). Cheese Wheat germ
Iodine	Stimulating to brain tissue	Deficiencies have been shown to lower IQ scores	Sea food, eggs and dairy
Vitamin C	Needed to make acetylcholine a brain chemical involved in memory	Lower immunity and slow wound healing. In its role in neurological support; Lacking concentration Inability to focus Mind wandering (day dreaming)	Broccoli, peppers, watercress, cabbage, cauliflower, strawberries, kiwi, tomatoes, citrus fruits, melon, peas
Vitamin B5	Needed to make acetylcholine a brain chemical involved in memory	Lacking concentration Inability to focus Mind wandering (day dreaming)	Mushrooms, avocados, eggs, peas, lentils, whole wheat, cabbage
Vitamin B1	Needed to make acetylcholine a brain chemical involved in memory	Lacking concentration Inability to focus Mind wandering (day dreaming)	Beans, peas, lamb, asparagus, watercress, mushrooms, cauliflower, Brussels, peppers, cabbage

Helping a child to concentrate, learn and remember (continued)

Nutrients needed	Role in Body	Deficiency Impact	Foods to include
Vitamin B12	Needed to make acetylcholine a brain chemical involved in memory	Lacking concentration Inability to focus Mind wandering (day dreaming)	Sardines, tuna, cottage cheese, turkey, chicken, egg yolks, milk, lamb
Phosphatidylserine (PS)	Helps neurons to communicate	Lacking concentration Inability to focus Mind wandering (day dreaming)	Soya, chicken, eggs, fish, beans and most types of meat.
Phosphatidlycholine (PCh)	Improves memory as PCh is the precurser of acetylcholine a brain chemical involved in memory.	Lacking concentration Inability to focus Mind wandering (day dreaming)	Egg yolks, soya beans, fish
Dimethylaminoethanol (DMAE)	Another precursor needed to make acetylcholine. DMAE can improve concentration, promote learning and stop the mind racing.	Lacking concentration Inability to focus Mind wandering (day dreaming)	Salmon anchovies and sardines
Pyroglutamate (PCA)	Yet another precursor of acetylcholine, improves communication between the left and right sides of the brain.	Slow reflexes. Lacking concentration Inability to focus Mind wandering (day dreaming)	Fruits, vegetables, meats fish and dairy products (unprocessed)

Helping a child's mood, behaviour and sleep

Nutrients needed	Role in Body	Deficiency Impact	Foods to include
Vitamin D	By absorbing calcium Vitamin D helps to build strong bones teeth & muscles. Also, an immune system modulator (increases or decreases immune function) Helps to convert tryptophan to serotonin hence the link with mood	Depression (low mood) Impact on immune function Weak bones	Sunlight! Play & activities outdoors give the best boost of vitamin D. Food sources; vitamin d enriched mushrooms, oily fish, egg yolks
Magnesium	Aids sleep & relaxation; positive affect on GABA (known as the "calming" neurotransmitter) Helps to produce serotonin Magnesium is essential for the relaxation of muscle fibres	Low levels of serotonin are associated with irritability, moodiness & depression.	Green leafy veg, brown rice, nuts, fish, meat, beans, wholemeal bread
Omega 3 & 6	Involved in brain growth & development. Needed to make eicosanoids – these help to keep inflammation down in the body	Systematic inflammation is linked to many chronic diseases including; heart disease, arthritis, diabetes & certain cancers.	Oily fish, mackerel, salmon, fresh tuna, sardines, fish oil. Egg yolks (Omega 3 enriched) Flax seeds chai seeds
Serotonin	Regulates mood, social behaviour, appetite, digestion, sleep & memory,	Linked to low mood & depression As serotonin is involved in the neurotransmitter melatonin, deficiencies in serotonin can adversely affect sleep.	Seaweed or more likely a spirulina supplement Light. Exercise/activity Food sources; eating tryptophan will convert to serotonin in the body. Tryptophan rich foods; salmon, eggs, seeds, nuts, chickpeas, cottage cheese, bananas.

General guide to using the recipes in this book

Bananas

When freezing, always peel first! Otherwise, it's an impossible task!

Eggs

Always use free range eggs. and perhaps try the 'Omega 3' enriched ones for additional nutrients

Measuring cups

As my cups are 250ml, my measuring is always based on 250ml. however, so long as you consistently use the same cup size within the recipe for all the ingredients that are measured in this way, the recipe will work.

Tuna

I opt for Albacore tuna as the fish is much nicer than generic tinned tuna. You will see the difference in colour, quality and taste. There are also more Omega 3 fatty acids, so the tuna sandwich becomes an even healthier option with Albacore!

Maple syrup

Always buy pure maple syrup; it is more expensive but the cheaper varieties contain invert sugar syrup

Vanilla Bean extract

When I refer to vanilla in recipes I am using vanilla bean extract, as with maple syrup some vanilla essence and extract can contain invert sugar syrup

Dried fruit

Always check that the fruit isn't sweetened, and check that sugar isn't listed in the ingredients - dried fruit should simply be dried fruit. Within the dried fruit section in shops you may find some products aimed at children masquerading as healthy, i.e. 'fruit shapes', but look carefully at the ingredients as some of these contain sugar, gelatine, palm oil and all sorts of other unnecessary ingredients.

Food Processor

I would be nowhere in the kitchen without my trusty processor! It isn't a fancy one just a small bowl mixer which grinds up nuts, grates carrots, blends soup and sauces, makes cakes, basically works very hard in my kitchen, they don't have to be expensive but are worth a little investment to save you a lot of time in the kitchen.

Hand-blender

My trusty hand-blender was a mere £5 many years ago but works wonders whizzing up milkshakes and giving soups a quick blend if you don't want to use the processor.

Chocolate and Cacao

When using chocolate I will always use dark with at least 70% cocoa content. For myself personally, I would always go for 85%, but this is likely to be too bitter for children. When using any powdered version I will always use raw cacao. Now there is more to the difference than a different way of spelling!

Cacao v cocoa

Raw cacao powder is made by cold-pressing unroasted cocoa beans. This process keeps the living enzymes in the cocoa and removes the fat (cacao butter).

Cocoa powder is raw cacao that's been roasted at high temperatures. Unfortunately roasting changes the molecular structure of the cocoa bean, reducing the enzyme content and lowering the overall nutritional value. Cocoa powder is what forms the base of processed chocolate bars/puddings, hot chocolates, spreads, cakes etc that you buy.

Cacao powder is known to have a higher antioxidant content than cocoa – and in its natural form Cacao is incredibly good for you, but when you see 'health benefits of chocolate', unless you're talking about 75-80% chocolate in shop-bought bars, or raw cacao, you're not getting those numerous health benefits.

Breakfasts

A high sugar breakfast can leave a child mentally and physically tired rather than energised for the day ahead. Keeping blood sugar levels stable will help the child to concentrate, and sneaking brain nutrients into breakfast and lunch boxes is a great way to boost their motivation, concentration and focus through the school day.

Breakfast options often marketed as healthy for children can contain a lot of added sugars, and this impacts on concentration. Initially, we may think that it will affect the child's behaviour, mood, attention and cognitive ability whilst at school and that this is short lived, but the nutritional impact goes a lot deeper.

Not so fun facts about sugar and IQ

Studies have shown a link between a poor diet associated with high fat, sugar and processed food content in early childhood may be attributed to small reductions in IQ in later childhood.

To maximise a child's mental performance, they need to have an even supply of glucose to the brain[1].

Research has found that dips in blood glucose are directly correlated to poor attention, poor memory and even aggressive behaviour.

Breakfast is a great way to start this blood glucose intake. These recipes all enable a slow release of energy that will see your child through the morning at school.

1. Dr David Benton Phd and Professor at Swansea University

Porridge

Porridge is a great way to start the day for the whole family, it is inexpensive and easy to prepare and fills everyone up with slow releasing energy. Many breakfast cereals will be full of added sugar and cause blood sugar to rise and then drop (probably during the first lesson at school which will affect concentration levels).

Banana, Honey & Almond Porridge

Plain porridge oats (I use 1 cup for 3 of us)
Almond milk (I use 3 cups)
1 banana
Sprinkle cinnamon
tsp honey

1. Mash banana in a bowl with the honey and cinnamon.
2. Make up your porridge with almond milk.
3. Mix together.

Apple & Sultana Porridge

1 apple diced
1 handful sultanas} This mixture will make enough for
two servings of apple porridge
tsp cinnamon
Tiny bit of butter
Plain porridge oats (I use 1 cup for 3 of us)
Almond milk (I use 3 cups)

1. In a pan heat the butter slowly adding the apple, sultanas and cinnamon.
2. Heat for 20 -30 minutes until the apple has softened.
3. Make up your porridge with almond milk.
4. Mix together.

There are many ways to experiment with porridge, I often use Cacao or Acai powder to give a boost of antioxidants - children will call these chocolate or purple porridge! You can also add in seeds such as milled flax seeds or chia seeds, barely noticeable by the child yet both are rich in ALA (Alpha-Linolenic Acid). The body can convert this into EPA and DHA, both of which have a positive impact on a child's developing brain.

Shop-bought Muesli and Granola can be a good substitute for making your own but the cheaper varieties are often loaded with added sugars and unnaturally sweet tasting. You can make your own according to your tastes. The following will give you a general idea, and hopefully the confidence to experiment! Adding dried fruit and the slightly sweeter 'soft' dried fruit adds a natural sweetness. Nuts and seeds add Omega 3 and are a good source of energy. If your muesli/granola is still not sweet enough when you serve, try adding some honey.

Home-made Muesli

1 cup almonds
1 cup macadamias
1 cup cashews
2 cups organic dried coconut flakes
½ cup pumpkin seeds
¼ cup chia seeds
1 tbsp ground cinnamon
1 tbsp ground ginger
60ml coconut oil

1. Preheat the oven to 350F/gas 4/180C (slightly less for fan assisted ovens).
2. Roughly chop all the nuts into chunky pieces.
3. Mix all of the dry ingredients in a bowl and mix well with the melted coconut oil.
4. Spread the muesli onto a baking tray lined with baking-paper.
5. Bake for 15 minutes until crispy and turning brown.
6. Allow to cool and store in an air-tight container.
(will keep for a few weeks, - if it lasts that long)
If you wish to add dried fruit this can be done when transferring the mix to the container after its baked, or at each serving. I personally much prefer it with the addition of dried fruit. (Check the dried fruit has not been coated in sugar).

Home-made Granola

4 cups Oats
1 ½ cups nuts and/or seeds (I like pecan nuts and
pumpkin seeds)
¼ cup coconut oil (melted)
¼ cup honey/maple syrup
Pinch cinnamon
1 tsp vanilla extract
1 cup dried fruit - (I like jumbo/golden raisins/pineapple
and pear)

1. Preheat the oven to 350F / gas 4 / 180C (slightly less for fan assisted ovens)
2. In a large mixing bowl combine the oats, nuts and / or seeds salt and cinnamon and blend well.
3. Add the melted oil, honey / maple syrup and vanilla; mix very well into the oat mixture.
4. Pour the granola mix onto a baking tray, spreading into an even layer.
5. Bake for about 25 minutes – check it halfway through.
6. Cool granola mix completely before adding the dried fruit.
7. Store in an air-tight container.
(will keep for a few weeks, - if it lasts that long)

Eggs

Eggs are great for adults and children alike – they are classified nutritionally as a complete protein source (they contain all essential amino acids).

Eggs are rich in brain nutrients including Phosphatidylcholine, Phosphatidylserine, vitamins B5 and B12.

In the nutrient table you will see how often eggs appear as a source of excellent nutrition.

Bacon and Egg Muffins

(not the fast food kind!)

Makes 12 muffins

12 slices high quality streaky bacon

12 large eggs

4 finely chopped spring onions

1 tsp smoked paprika

Chives to serve

1. Preheat the oven to moderate 175 180C, (gas 4, 350F).
2. Use a silicone muffin tray (x 12 or 2x6) and line each one with baking paper.
3. Use the bacon to line the muffins - make a ring with two slices of bacon.
4. Bake in the oven for about 10 minutes or until the bacon looks crisp.
5. Meanwhile, crack the eggs in a large jug and add the spring onion and mix well.
6. Pour the mixture over the bacon baskets.
7. Dust each basket with paprika.
8. Bake in the oven for 25 minutes.
9. Garnish with the chives.

Banana Pancakes

(Serves 1)

1 banana

½ tsp ground cinnamon

½ tbsp. almond butter

2 eggs

1 tbsp coconut oil

1. Put the banana, cinnamon, almond butter and eggs in a blender. Blend until well mixed and fluffy.
2. Place a large pan on medium heat and add the coconut oil. Once hot slowly add the pancake mixture to the pan.
3. When bubbles start to form on the surface flip the pancake and cook the second side.

Suggested toppings: -

Berries

Chopped bananas and walnuts

Tuna Cakes

Makes 12

3 tbsp melted butter

Canned albacore tuna in water, drained

3 spring onions, thinly sliced

1⅓ cup mashed baked sweet potato

Finely grated zest from ½ medium lemon

2 large eggs

Freshly ground black pepper

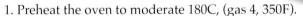

1. Preheat the oven to moderate 180C, (gas 4, 350F).
2. Grease a 12-cup regular sized muffin tin or silicone muffin tray with **one** tablespoon of melted butter.
3. In a large bowl, mix together the tuna and spring onions.
4. Add the cooked mashed sweet potato to the tuna mixture, and gently combine.
5. Mix in the lemon zest, the remaining two tablespoons of butter, and the eggs.
7. Season with salt and pepper to taste.
8. Scoop a quarter cup of the mixture into each greased muffin tin cup and flatten with the back of a spoon.
9. Bake the tuna cakes for 20-25 minutes
10. Transfer the cakes to a wire rack to cool.

These 'cakes' can be stored in an air-tight container in the fridge for 3-4 days.

These are ideal SCHOOL LUNCH BOX OPTIONS

Courgette and Sun-dried Tomato Muffins

Makes 6 muffins

Coconut oil for greasing

1½ cups grated courgette

Sun-dried tomatoes, rinsed if in oil

1 medium clove garlic

½ cup pumpkin seeds

2 eggs

2 heaped tablespoons flaxseed meal

¼ cup tapioca flour

½ tsp onion powder

¼ tsp baking powder

1. Preheat the oven to moderate 180C, (gas 4, 350F).
2. Grease a muffin tray (6 casings) with a little coconut oil.
3. Using your hands, squeeze grated courgette to remove as much of the juice as possible. Add the flesh to a mixing bowl.
4. Add sun-dried tomatoes, garlic and pumpkin seeds to a food processor. Process until ground and incorporated. Transfer to the bowl with the grated courgette.
5. Add eggs, flaxseed meal, tapioca flour, onion powder, and baking powder to the mix, and mix well.
6. Divide the mixture between 6 muffin casings and place in the oven, middle shelf.
7. Bake for 30-35 minutes. Remove and set aside to cool completely before removing from the tray.

These muffins can be stored in an air-tight container in the fridge for 3-4 days.

These are ideal SCHOOL LUNCH BOX OPTIONS

I would always recommend using free range, Omega 3 enriched eggs.

Spreads & 'Jams'

Toast/sandwiches can be very appealing to young children and are great ways to get them to eat. However, as with most things, often the jars and fillings marketed for young children are perhaps not as nutritious as they could be.

Here are some recipes to encourage you to try making your own toast toppings, (they also make ideal lunchtime sandwich fillings), and some fun ways to engage your little ones and get creative with food.

Cacao Hazelnut Spread

1 avocado

1 cup blanched hazelnuts

1 tbsp raw cacao powder

60ml maple syrup

1. Roast the blanched hazelnuts in the oven for 10-12 minutes, do not allow them to burn.
2. Add the nuts to a food processor and blitz until they form a paste.
3. Add in the remaining ingredients and blitz to your desired consistency.
4. Store in the fridge for 4-5 days.

Unlike the shop-bought variety, this contains no added sugar but is full of healthy fats from the avocado and antioxidants from the cacao.

Peanut Chocolate Butter

1 cup unsalted peanuts

50g 70% dark chocolate melted

2 tbsp maple syrup

1 tsp vanilla

1 tbsp hazelnut oil

1. Roast the nuts on low heat for 8-10 minutes.
2. Transfer to a food processor and blitz.
3. Add the melted chocolate, vanilla and maple syrup and process until smooth and creamy.
4. Store in the fridge in an airtight jar or container.

Sesame Nut Butter

1 cup unsalted cashew nuts

¼ cup unsweetened desiccated coconut

½ cup sesame seeds

1 tbsp melted coconut oil

1. Roast the nuts and seeds on a low heat for 8-10 minutes.
2. Melt the coconut oil.
3. Add everything to a food processor and blitz, it may take a while to get a consistency you like.
4. Store in the fridge in an airtight container or jar for 5-6 days.

Nut Butter

1 cup unsalted almonds

¾ cup unsalted walnuts

1 tbsp maple syrup

1 tbsp vanilla

1. Roast the nuts on low heat for 8-10 minutes.
2. Transfer to a food processor and blitz.
   Add the vanilla and maple syrup and process until smooth and creamy.
3. Store in the fridge in an airtight jar or container for 5-6 days.

Apricot Spread

½ cup soft dried apricots
½ cup pitted dates
1 tbsp maple syrup
100ml cold water

1. Place all ingredients in a pan on a low heat for 20-25 minutes, keep an eye on it adding a little more water if you need to, give it long enough to thicken and look sticky.
2. Allow to cool slightly.
3. Transfer to food processor and blitz until smooth.
4. Store in the fridge in an airtight jar or container for 5-6 days.

Strawberry 'Jam'

250ml water
1 tsp agar flakes (vegan algae-based setting agent)
100g soft dried strawberries
1 tsp maple syrup

1. Mix agar flakes in water.
2. Add strawberries to pan.
3. Cover with the water, agar mix and heat gently.
4. Add maple syrup.
5. Keep on a medium heat for 20 minutes, keeping an eye on it and allowing it to thicken.
6. Transfer to food processor and blitz until smooth.
7. Store in the fridge in an airtight jar or container for 5-6 days.

Lunch

If your child has lunch at school it can be hard to tell how much they have eaten or whether they avoided all the veg. This is their first real taste of food freedom; they get to pick and no one is there nagging at them to eat everything. They also get to eat pudding regardless of whether they ate their lunch!

53

School lunches can be a great choice for children and great steps have been taken into better sourcing of ingredients; more foods are cooked on site and there are now healthier options. If you have any concerns about the food provision at your child's school a conversation with the school is acceptable, they are your children after all!

If you choose to provide packed lunches instead you do have more elements of control; but, whilst you can control what you put in their packed lunch, you cannot stop them swapping!

Packed lunches can be good if you have very picky eaters and worry that they genuinely won't eat the school menu available, that's certainly better than them going hungry.

Water should always be the drink of choice in a packed lunch, as mentioned previously plain water is essential to brain function and should always be available as a first-choice drink.

Making a school lunch fun, appetising and nutritious every day can be a bit challenging, there are some good ways to try to get children to engage more with their lunch by making it fun.

- For younger children sandwiches can be cut into shapes using biscuit cutters

- Aim for a mix of sweet and savoury items

- Go for smaller portions and more choice rather than one giant sandwich, they are more likely to eat a bit of each thing rather than all of one thing.

Check out the dips and sandwich fillings in the lunch recipe
section for more ideas on lunch box fillers and look out for the
lunch box icon.

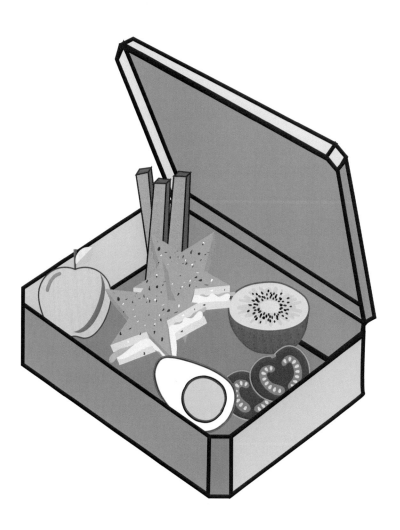

Scrummy Sandwich Fillings

I do not know any small children who do not like a sandwich!

These suggestions can be used on:

Whole-wheat bread/wraps/pitta breads, for lunch boxes

Crackers or toast for a lunch at home

Any of the following fillings can be made and kept for 2-3 days.

Cheese, Apple/Carrot/Celery with Yogurt

Grated mature cheese

Grated apple/celery/carrot (one of them or any combination)

2-3 tbsp natural yogurt

Simply mix everything together ready to spoon into the wraps.

Having cheese with grated fruit and veg still meets your cheese need but adds in bulk via other foods thus reducing the quantity of cheese consumed and giving you some added nutrients, taste and texture.

Tuna and Avocado

1 avocado mashed with a fork
1/3 jar Albacore tuna mashed with a fork
1 tbsp full fat Greek yogurt

Simply mash the avocado and tuna together with the spoon of Greek yogurt. This will keep in the fridge for 2 days but the avocado may discolour.

Tuna and Egg Mayonnaise

1 hard-boiled egg mashed
1/3 jar Albacore tuna mashed with a fork
1 tsp Mayonnaise

Simply mix everything all together.

If you want to make your own mayonnaise here is a simple recipe, as long as the eggs are produced under the British Lion Code of Practice they are safe for children to eat raw. However, avoid raw or lightly cooked eggs if you are using eggs that are not British Lion stamped, i.e., not hen eggs, (such as duck, quail), or any eggs from outside of the UK.

Home-made Mayonnaise

1 egg at room temperature

2 tbsp lemon juice

½ tsp Dijon-style mustard or mustard powder

½ tsp salt

300ml extra light olive oil

1. Into a large jug add the egg, lemon juice, mustard, salt and 60ml of the olive oil. Using a hand blender blend until ingredients have combined.
2. Add the remaining olive oil and blend until the ingredients have formed an emulsion.
3. Transfer to a sterilised jar and refrigerate, this will keep for one week.

Chicken, Walnut & Grape

Left-over roast chicken
Handful of walnuts crushed
Handful of either purple grapes or sultanas
2 tbsp natural yogurt

1. Shred the roast chicken.
2. Add the crushed walnuts to the natural yogurt and stir.
3. Dice the grapes so that each grape is in about 8 pieces (if using sultanas you can leave them as they are).
4. Add the grapes to the yogurts and walnuts.
5. Add the chicken giving it all a good mix.

Salmon & Green Salad Vegetables

Poached salmon (good to save some from the night before
so that sandwiches are quick and easy to make)
baby spinach (chopped)
Avocado mashed
Couple of spoons of natural yogurt or Greek yogurt

1. Flake the poached salmon taking extra care to ensure no bones.
2. Add all ingredients to the yogurt and give a good mix.

Peanut Butter and Banana

You can use any of the suggested nut butters in the spread section, add some sliced banana in the sandwich or mash it in, this will be particularly filling but a very nutritious lunch full of EFA's.

Not Jam

Use the fruit spread recipe for a not-so-sugary jam sandwich.

If you are at home the following options work well (but they would be unsuitable to pack away into lunch boxes).

Satay Chicken Wrap

Cooked/leftover roast chicken
2 tbsp satay sauce - see page 86
Grated carrot
Grated courgette
Shredded red/white or both cabbage

Simply place all together folding up the wrap at the bottom to avoid spillage.

Tuna and Cheese Melt

¼ jar albacore tuna mashed and mixed with the mayonnaise
½ cup grated cheddar cheese
1 tsp mayonnaise
Thick slice wholemeal bread

1. Place bread under a grill and toast on one side.
2. Remove, and onto the untoasted side add the tuna mix, then cover with the grated cheese.
3. Return to the grill, until the cheese has melted.

Chicken and Broccoli Parcels

Left-over roast chicken
Steamed broccoli flaked very small
Grated cheddar cheese
1 tbsp Greek yogurt

1. Shred the roast chicken.
2. Flake the broccoli and combine all ingredients.
3. Serve warm in a wrap rolled up.

Rainbow Vegetables Wrap with Hummus

Grated carrot
Grated courgette
Shredded red cabbage
2 tbsp hummus (see recipe in the dip section)

1. Get the veg as small as you can.
2. Combine with the hummus, and roll up in a wrap.

Dips

These dips are great for snacking, adding to lunches or mixing up sandwiches.

Pea and Mint Dip

400g frozen peas, defrosted
100g full fat Greek yogurt
1 tsp ground cumin
Squeeze fresh lemon juice
Small handful mint leaves

1. Whizz the peas, yogurt, lemon juice, cumin, and mint together in a food processor to a texture you like.
2. This can be served straight away in a serving bowl, or kept in small tubs in the fridge for you to take out and about.

Hummus

1 tin chickpeas rinsed

2 tbsp tahini paste (a sesame seed paste)

1 tsp garlic puree or 1 fresh garlic clove pressed/grated

2 tsp fresh lemon juice

½ tsp ground cumin

½ tsp smoked paprika

4-7 tbsp water (you will know as you mix whether it
needs more or less)

1. Rinse the chickpeas.
2. Place all ingredients into the processor except the water.
3. Blend slowly.
4. Add the water gradually, you will see if you need more
   or less by the way the dip looks.
5. Can be used straight away or kept in the fridge for 4-5
   days in an air-tight container.

Pesto Dips

Use the pesto recipes to make a quick and tasty dip. It's
worth making extra pesto to make a dip for lunch the
following day.

Not Guacamole

Although this is by no means a traditional guacamole recipe it is a great tasty, creamy way for kids to enjoy avocado.

1-2 ripe avocados

100g full fat natural yogurt

1 tsp smoked paprika

Mash the avocado with a fork until smooth, spoon in the yogurt and stir, finally adding in the smoked paprika.

Home-made Salsa

4 ripe tomatoes finely chopped

8 sprigs coriander finely chopped

¼ onion finely chopped

Green chilli (optional)

Juice and zest of a lime

Simply mix all together.

Red Lentil, Squash and Yogurt Dip

¼ butternut squash
1 carrot
½ cup red lentils rinsed thoroughly
1 tsp garlic puree
1 tsp ground cumin
1 tsp tomato puree
Squeeze of lemon juice
1 tsp rapeseed oil
Drizzle of honey

1. Chop the squash and carrot into small chunks and put on to steam for 10-12 minutes or until feel soft.
2. Meanwhile place the lentils in a saucepan cover with water and bring to the boil before reducing to a medium heat for 20 minutes.
3. Heat a small pan on a low heat and heat the garlic and tomato puree, add the squash and carrot and lightly stir fry until coated in the garlic and tomato, add the cumin – remove from the heat.
4. Once the lentils are soft to the touch place in a food processor - I use a skimmer spoon to avoid any excess water.
5. Add the squash and carrot mixture to the processor.
6. Blitz then add the lemon juice.
7. Blitz again, once it is a fairly smooth consistency it is ready to transfer to a bowl and add the honey.

Yogurt and Cucumber Dip

Greek yogurt
½ cucumber finely diced
Squeeze of lemon juice

1. Dice cucumber.
2. Add to yogurt.
3. Squeeze in lemon juice.

Soups

Broccoli and Cheese Soup

1 head of broccoli chopped (stalk included)
1 onion
1 medium sized potato diced
4 cups chicken or vegetable stock
2 cups of grated cheese or 1 small block of stilton
Olive Oil
Black pepper to taste

1. In a Wok stir fry the onion until soft then add the potato and cook for another 5 minutes.
2. Add the stock and reduce the heat.
3. When simmering add the broccoli – cook for 20 minutes.
4. Remove from the heat and blend.
5. Add the cheese and give one more quick blitz with the blender.
6. Season to taste.

Coconut Pumpkin Soup

1 diced onion
1cm fresh ginger finely grated
1 garlic clove
1 pumpkin (butternut squash) diced
1 tbsp coconut oil
1 litre vegetable stock
½ can coconut cream

1. In a large saucepan over a medium heat add the onion, ginger and garlic to the coconut oil, and fry for few minutes.
2. Add the pumpkin and stir for another 2 minutes.
3. Add the stock and bring to the boil.
4. Reduce to a simmer and cook for 20 minutes or until the pumpkin is soft.
5. Once slightly cooler blend until smooth and creamy.
6. Stir in the coconut cream and serve.

Carrot, Lentil and Honey soup

6 carrots chopped
1 leak sliced and rinsed
1 cup red lentils rinsed
500ml vegetable stock add more or less as you need
1 tbsp honey
1 knob of butter
1 tbsp crème fraiche to swirl in to the finished soup

1. Melt the butter in a large pan.
2. Add the leeks and cook on a medium heat until soft.
3. Add the carrots and lentils then cover with the stock.
4. Reduce heat to a simmer for 35-40 minutes until the lentils are soft.
5. Use a hand blender or food processor to blend the soup.
6. Pour back into the pan and add the honey, its then ready to serve.
7. Add a swirl of crème fraiche to each bowl as you serve.

Can be frozen in batches (don't add the crème fraiche if freezing).

Creamy Chicken Soup

1 large carrot diced

1 leek chopped and rinsed

2 potatoes diced

2 sticks celery diced

2 knobs butter

2 tbsp plain flour

700ml chicken stock

150ml milk

2 cooked chicken breasts or leftover roast chicken

2 tbsp single cream

2 knobs butter

1. Using a large pan, melt the butter and add the veg, keep on a low heat.
2. Cover the veg with the flour and cook for a further 5 minutes before adding the stock and milk.
3. Bring the pan to the boil then reduce to a simmer.
4. Simmer for 25 – 30 minutes until the vegetables are soft, add the cooked chicken.
5. Transfer to a food processor to blend.
6. Pour back into the pan and swirl in the cream before serving.

Creamy Tomato and Basil Soup

500ml passata
1 tin chopped/plum tomatoes
2 veg stock cubes (not mixed with water)
3 tbsp double cream
Bunch basil chopped

1. Add all ingredients except the cream into a saucepan.
2. Heat on a medium heat for 25 minutes.
3. Transfer to a food processor and blend.
4. Return to the pan and add the double cream before serving.

Other lunches that are quick and easy to make are jacket potatoes or jacket sweet potatoes. You can use some of the sandwich fillings as potato toppings, or the home-made baked beans (see page 116) and cheese.

Dinner time

Dinner time can be a great way for the family to spend time together, though I know this can sometimes prove to be tricky with work commitments and after school activities. However, it is good to try to sit down as a family as often as possible to eat together.

Children are very much led by parental influence, and this is no different when it comes to food. If you are seen to have a good relationship with food and willingly eat and enjoy healthy food, children will view that as the norm. Similarly, if as parents you often eat high sugar, high fat foods, you will be setting a different 'norm' for your children.

Parental influence with food goes a lot deeper; if a parent is seen to be constantly on a diet or trying to lose weight by eating different foods, children will start to see this as normal. This can have a potentially damaging effect on children's view of food in relation to body image.

In this section you will find a variety of easy to prepare meals, ways to hide vegetables and theme nights which makes eating more of an experience, and an opportunity to explore both new foods and different cultures.

Dinner Recipes

Pasta – often a staple favourite but how can you make it more exciting and more nutritious?

Making your own pesto and pasta sauces is a good way to start, as you can add in additional vegetables but lose the added sugar content often put into jars.

My favourite pasta sauce is the hidden vegetable sauce on page 111. I make this once a week.

Roasted Tomato, Spinach and Mascarpone Sauce

Large bowl of cherry tomatoes
Bag of baby spinach or a cup of frozen spinach
Handful of torn basil leaves
1 clove garlic - grated/pressed
½ tub mascarpone cheese

1. Place the tomatoes in an oven-proof dish and slow roast in the oven for 30 mins at 160C/140C fan/320F/gas 3.
2. When the tomatoes are roasted, allow to cool before transferring to a food processor (or a large bowl with a hand-blender).
3. Add the spinach, basil, garlic and mascarpone and whizz up until you have a smooth looking sauce.
4. Heat gently in a pan and serve with your choice of pasta.

Green Pesto

1 bag basil
½ bag spinach
¼ block parmesan
Small cup pine nuts
¼ cup olive oil
Pinch black pepper

You can bash it all away in a pestle and mortar, or give it a quick blitz in a processor and you're done!

Red Pesto

1 bag basil
¼ block parmesan
Small cup pine nuts
¼ cup olive oil
Pinch black pepper
½ cup sun blush tomatoes

As above

To change either of the above into a dip - stir a few spoons into full fat Greek Yogurt.

Kale Pesto

½ bag kale (remove rough stalks)
¼ block parmesan
Small cup pine nuts
Juice ½ lemon
1 clove garlic (leave this out if you don't like garlic, as it
is raw and tastes very garlic-y!)
¼ cup olive oil

Simply blitz all the ingredients together and there's
your pesto!

Avocado and Cashew Pesto

1 ripe avocado
1 slice lemon
2 inch block parmesan
Handful mint leaves
Small cup cashew nuts

Blitz the nuts first until they look more like a smooth
paste, add the remaining ingredients and blitz away.

Roasted Red Pepper and Walnut Pesto

1 red pepper
1 bunch basil
2 inch block parmesan
½ cup olive oil
8-10 walnuts

1. Roast the red pepper in the oven at 180C/160C fan/350F/gas 4 for 30 minutes until soft.
2. Blitz the walnuts until crumbled up, then add the remaining ingredients and blitz away.
3. For a lovely creamy dip stir in some soft-cheese.

Remember the hidden vegetable pasta sauce? This is great to make once a week and use for any pasta dish.
See page 111

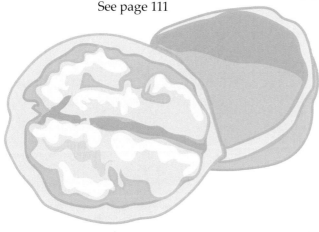

Butternut Squash, Mushroom and Spinach Lasagne

Butternut squash lasagne sheets

1 pack chestnut mushrooms

2 cups sun blush tomatoes

1 cup ricotta cheese

1 bag baby spinach

2 garlic cloves pressed/grated

Mozzarella and parmesan cheese to top

Black pepper

Pinch nutmeg

1 tsp olive oil

1. In a small pan gently heat the olive oil and add half the garlic.
2. Add the mushrooms and cover - leave for 10 minutes.
3. In another pan wilt the spinach with the other half of garlic.
4. Take the wilted spinach and mix with the ricotta cheese, black pepper and nutmeg.
5. Mix together the mushrooms, spinach and tomatoes in a bowl (or one of the pans).
6. Start with a layer of the mushroom and spinach mixture in your lasagne dish.
7. Add a layer of butternut squash sheets.
8. Add the remaining mushroom mixture.
9. Top with a layer of butternut squash sheets.
10. Add the mozzarella and parmesan, making sure you cover the top completely.
11. Bake on a low heat (150C / 130C fan / 300F / gas 2) for at least one hour, then turn up the heat / grill for 10 minutes.

Lentil Bolognese

1 tbsp olive oil

2 onions finely chopped

3 carrots finely chopped

3 celery sticks finely chopped

3 garlic cloves, crushed

500g bag dried red lentils

2 x 400g cans chopped tomatoes

2 tbsp tomato purée

2 tsp dried oregano

2 tsp dried basil

3 bay leaves

1 litre vegetable stock

500g wholewheat spaghetti,

Parmesan or vegetarian cheese, grated, to serve

1. Heat the oil in a large saucepan and add the onions, carrots, celery and garlic.
2. Cook gently for 15-20 mins until everything is softened.
3. Stir in the lentils, chopped tomatoes, tomato purée, herbs and stock.
4. Bring to a simmer and cook for 40-50 mins until the lentils are tender and saucy - splash in water if you need to.
5. If eating straight away, keep on a low heat while you cook the spaghetti, following the pack instructions.
6. Drain well; divide the spaghetti between pasta bowls or plates, then spoon the sauce over the top and grate on some cheese.
7. Alternatively, cool the sauce and chill for up to 3 days. Or freeze for up to 3 months. Simply defrost portions overnight at room temperature, and reheat gently to serve.

Fish Dishes

You will see oily fish appearing lots of times in the nutrients table. Here are some ways to hopefully make family friendly fish recipes.

Easy Peasy Fish Pie

Salmon fillets

Jar albacore tuna

Milk (to poach fish)

Peas

Sweetcorn

Potatoes - peeled and chopped

Carrots - peeled and chopped

Cheese - enough to grate and cover the oven-proof dish

(use red cheese if you really want to hide the carrot in

the mash)

4 tsp cornflour to thicken sauce

1. In one pan pour in enough milk to cover the salmon fillets and simmer gently (do not boil) for 20-35 minutes.
2. In another pan add the potatoes and carrots and bring to the boil, then reduce to a simmer until soft enough to mash.
3. Meanwhile, steam the peas and sweetcorn.
4. Remove the salmon and flake into an oven-proof dish (keeping the milk to one side for now).

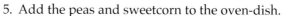

5. Add the peas and sweetcorn to the oven-dish.
6. Add the jar of tuna.
7. Mash the potatoes and carrots together.
8. Go back to the milk pan (removing any fish skins etc.).
9. Turn the heat back on a low heat.
10. Stir in half the grated cheese and cornflour, and stir continually until you have a cheese sauce.
11. Add the cheese sauce to the oven dish, cover with the mashed potato and carrot and then the grated cheese.
12. Transfer to the oven for 30 mins at 190C/170C fan/ 375F/gas 5.

Mackerel Pate

Cooked mackerel fillets - take care to remove all bones

½ tub soft cheese

½ tub Greek yogurt

Squeeze of lime juice

1. Flake the mackerel fillets, being really careful to remove all bones.
2. Add to a processor.
   Squeeze in the lime juice.
3. Add the soft cheese and Greek yogurt and blitz to your desired consistency.

This pate is a great way to get children to eat oily fish, as mackerel tends to have quite a strong fishy taste that can put some children off. This pate makes it creamy and more palatable to children. Serve on wholemeal toast or with Pitta breads with thin cucumber slices.

Fish Fingers

2 white fish fillets skinned and care taken to remove bones

1 beaten egg

50g breadcrumbs

2 tbsp plain flour

1 tsp coconut flour

1. Cut the fish into sections.
2. Coat in the flour (covering both sides of the fish finger).
3. Dunk the floured fish into the beaten egg.
4. Next coat them in the breadcrumbs, giving them a good covering.
5. Heat the coconut oil in a frying pan on a medium heat.
6. Add the fish - take care not to over-turn them.
7. They should be cooked within 8-10 minutes depending on the size.

Fish fingers of course go well with mashed potatoes and peas or chips! For extra nutrients try mashing some vegetables in with your potato, or making sweet potato chips instead!

This can be fun for children to help with, but it is also quite messy!!

Salmon Fish Cakes

2-3 salmon fillets (or a tin of red salmon)

2 -3 potatoes cooked and mashed

½ butternut squash cooked and mashed

Cup sweetcorn

Cup peas

1 large beaten egg

50g breadcrumbs

2 tbsp plain flour

1 tsp coconut flour

1. Cook and mash the potatoes and squash and put to one side - cooler mash is easier to work with!
2. Whilst the potatoes are cooking cook the salmon in the oven - under foil/baking paper for 15 mins at 180C/160C fan/350F/gas 4.
3. Flake the salmon and place in a bowl, taking care to remove any bones.
4. Add in the mashed potato and mashed squash, peas and sweetcorn and give it all a good mix.
5. Mould the mixture into fish cake sizes.
6. Dip each fish cake into the flour first, then the egg and finally the breadcrumbs.
7. Heat the coconut oil in a frying pan on a medium heat.
8. Add the fish cakes - take care not to over-turn them.
9. They should be cooked within 8-10 minutes depending on the size.

As above, fish cakes are great with mash or chips!

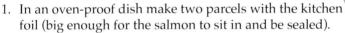

Other great ways to eat fish (without hiding it):

Thai Style Parcels

2 Salmon fillets

Red chilli finely chopped (optional if children don't like the heat)

Fresh ginger grated - to your taste

Finely sliced spring onion

Lime, zested and juiced

Kaffir lime leaves (available in Asian supermarkets, I use frozen)

Baby corn

Tender-stem broccoli

Coconut block

Brown rice

Kitchen foil/baking paper

1. In an oven-proof dish make two parcels with the kitchen foil (big enough for the salmon to sit in and be sealed).
2. Place each salmon fillet in the foil parcel.
3. Add the chopped red chilli, spring onion and grated ginger – rubbing in a little.
4. Grate and juice the lime, rubbing the zest in and squeezing the juice over.
5. Scatter a few kaffir lime leaves and seal the individual bags.
6. Oven-cook at 180C / 160C fan / 350F / gas 4 for 20-25 minutes, according to the size of the salmon fillets.
7. Cook the rice as per the packet instructions; when cooked take off the heat and crumble in about a third of a coconut block, stir through until it has melted.
8. Meanwhile steam the baby corn and broccoli (they are best firm, so keep an eye on how long you cook them for).

Sesame Tuna & Home-Made Egg Fried Rice

Tuna steaks 1 or ½ per person

Grated ginger

Sesame oil

3 eggs

Brown rice

Frozen peas

Soy sauce

Pak choi

Red & orange/yellow peppers

Bean sprouts

1. In an oven-proof dish make two parcels with the kitchen foil (big enough for the tuna to sit in and be sealed).
2. Place the tuna steaks in, pouring over a drizzle of sesame oil and the grated ginger, rubbing the ginger in before sealing the parcel.
3. Oven cook the tuna for 8-12 minutes (I do it for longer but some people like it still quite pink, cook to your tastes).
4. Serve with the home-made egg fried rice and stir-fried vegetables.
5. Cook the rice according to the packet instructions.
6. Make scrambled eggs with the 3 eggs and add to the cooked rice.
7. Stir in the frozen peas to the cooked rice and egg mixture.
8. Add a splash of soy sauce.
9. Stir fry the peppers and pak choi for a few minutes, leaving firm then add beansprouts at the very last minute.

Curries

Satay Sauce with Veg Ribbons

Satay sauce
1 tsp coconut oil
1-2 tsp red Thai curry paste (make it very mild or as hot as you like, depending on your family's taste)
Tin coconut milk
Splash soy sauce
2-3 tbsp peanut butter
2-3 tbsp coconut sugar
2-3 tbsp peanuts (crushed for serving)
2 -3 carrots spiralised
2-4 courgettes spiralised
½ red cabbage chopped into long thin ribbons

1. In a medium pan heat the coconut oil and curry paste
2. Add the tin of coconut milk, make sure the pan is on a low heat.
3. Add the peanut butter, soy sauce and coconut sugar, stir frequently keeping the heat low.
4. Gradually the sauce will thicken, once it has move to one side.
5. Spiralise the vegetables and chop the red cabbage, spread them all out in a large serving bowl.
6. Blitz the peanuts up in a processor or use a pestle and mortar to crush them.
7. Drizzle the sauce over the veg dish and sprinkle the peanuts over the top.

I would recommend this with the chicken dippers on page 95

Creamy apricot and squash Korma – use Chicken/Tofu

Jar of mild korma paste
½ butternut squash
1 Cup dried apricots
Tin coconut milk
1 Cup frozen peas
Brown rice

1. In a large pan add the squash, curry paste, apricots and coconut milk simmer gently until the squash is soft.
2. If using chicken place chicken breast in an oven-proof dish cover with baking paper and a drizzle of oil and roast in the oven until cooked. (If using Tofu heat a tsp coconut oil and gently stir fry the tofu).
3. Remove from the heat and blitz the sauce up with a hand blender/food processor.
4. Add the chicken/Tofu to the sauce once it has been blitzed.
5. Cook the brown rice according to the packet. instructions and cook some frozen peas to add to the rice.

Mango, Coconut Curry with Diced Salmon/White Fish/ Diced Chicken/Tofu Cubes

Bag baby spinach or 1 cup of frozen spinach

½ butternut squash chopped

1 cup frozen mango

1-2 carton coconut cream, or a tin of coconut milk

Brown rice

Frozen Peas

1 teaspoon Red Thai Curry Paste

1. Add the chopped squash to a steamer or simmer in a pan until nearly soft, add the spinach and mango for the last 5-6 mins of cooking.
2. Drain the squash, spinach and mango, place in a bowl with the coconut cream and Curry paste to blitz with a hand blender or process in a food processor until a creamy blended sauce.
3. Transfer the blended sauce to an oven-proof dish - cook on a low to moderate heat (180C/160C fan/350F/gas 4) in the oven for 20-30 minutes with your choice of protein, making sure you have chopped these quite small for faster cooking, and check regularly.
4. Cook the brown rice as per the packet instructions.
5. Remove from the oven and serve with brown rice with cooked peas.

Vegetable Thai Curry

2 tsps coconut oil
1 tbsp red Thai curry paste
½ butternut squash chopped into bite-sized chunks
2 carrots chopped small
1 sweet potato chopped small
1 aubergine chopped small
1 yellow pepper finely sliced
1 red pepper finely sliced
1 bag baby spinach
1 tin coconut milk (you will need two tins if you increase the vegetable content to freeze half)
1/2 pint vegetable stock

1. Heat the coconut oil in a large pan and add the curry paste.
2. Add the squash, carrots and sweet potato.
3. Coat in the curry paste then add the stock.
4. Simmer for 15 minutes.
5. Add the aubergine and coconut milk and simmer for a further 10 minutes.
6. Add the peppers and simmer for another 15 minutes.
7. Add the spinach stir in for a further 5 minutes checking that the root veg is soft to the touch.
8. If you need to you can blend the sauce at this stage to hide all the vegetables.

There are lots of variations to the Thai curry: -

Chicken breasts/thighs   *Beef*
Quorn pieces   *Tofu*
Prawns

Root Vegetable, Lentil and Pineapple Curry

1 red onion	1 tin coconut milk
1 stick celery	2 tins chopped tomatoes
½ aubergine	3-4 tbsp Balti curry paste
¼ butternut squash	¼ pineapple
1 small potato	1 tsp garlic puree
3-4 carrots	1 tsp tomato puree
Green beans	1 tsp coconut oil
1 cup rinsed red lentils	

1. Chop all the vegetables, including the pineapple, into bite sized pieces.
2. Heat the coconut oil and add the garlic and tomato paste.
3. Add the red onion for 2-3 minutes then the celery for a further 3-4 minutes.
4. Add the curry paste.
5. Add all of the chopped vegetables, stirring well to cover in paste.
6. Turn down the heat and stir for a few minutes adding the tomatoes and coconut milk.
7. Add the rinsed lentils and pineapple and simmer for 2-3 hours, stirring occasionally.
8. Alternatively, you can transfer it to the oven at this stage on a low heat (about 150C/130 fan/300F/gas 2).

Sweet Potato, Spinach and Lentil Dahl

Either as a main meal with pitta, or as a side dish with other curries

100g red lentils

450ml vegetable stock

1 small finely chopped onion

2 tomatoes chopped

1/2 tsp turmeric

1 tsp garam masala

1 red chilli finely chopped

1 large sweet potato cut into small pieces

Large handful of young leaf spinach washed and shredded

1. Put all of the ingredients (excluding the sweet potato and spinach) into a pan, bring to a simmer and cook for 20 minutes.
2. Add the sweet potato and cook for a further 14 minutes or until tender, finally stir in the spinach, allow it to wilt (2-3 mins max) and serve!

Yogurt and Cucumber Dip

Greek yogurt

½ cucumber finely diced

Squeeze of lemon juice

Dice cucumber. Add to yogurt. Squeeze in lemon juice.

Fast Food not Junk Food

Vegan Burgers

1 tin of chickpeas
1 tin of sweetcorn
½ tsp ground coriander
½ tsp ground cumin
Zest of 1 lemon
3 heaped tbsp plain flour, (plus extra for dusting)
rapeseed oil
1 small round lettuce
2 large ripe tomatoes
tomato ketchup - see recipe on page 117
4 wholemeal burger buns

1. Drain and place both the chickpeas and sweetcorn into a food processor.
2. Add the spices, lemon zest, flour and a pinch of salt, then pulse until combined, - but not smooth - you want to retain a bit of texture.
3. On a flour-dusted surface, divide and shape the mixture into four equally sized patties (roughly 2cm thick).
4. Pop onto a tray and place in the fridge for around 30 minutes to firm up.
5. Heat a splash of oil in a large frying pan over a medium heat.

6. Once hot, add the patties and cook for around 10 minutes, or until golden and cooked through, turning halfway.
7. Meanwhile, wash and dry four lettuce leaves, then finely slice the tomatoes
8. Top with the burgers. Layer over a couple of slices of tomato, a lettuce leaf and burger tops.

Beef Burgers

400g lean minced beef

1 onion diced

1 clove garlic pressed/grated

2 tbsp fresh parsley chopped

1 large egg beaten

2 tbsp rapeseed oil

1. Heat ½ the oil to sweat off the onion and garlic.
2. In a bowl simply add all the mince, parsley, egg and the softened onion and garlic.
3. Mix well with your hands and shape into 4 large, or 8 small burgers.
4. Heat the remaining oil in the pan and fry in batches until cooked all the way through.

Chick Pea Burgers

Tin chick peas

1 carrot (grated)

1 courgette (grated)

1 garlic clove pressed/grated

1 tsp ground cumin

1 large egg beaten

2 tbsp plain flour

1 tbsp rapeseed oil

1. Drain and rinse the chick peas.
2. Add the chick peas, garlic, grated carrots, courgettes and cumin to a food processor and blitz.
3. Add the beaten egg and flour and mix again.
4. Make burger shapes out of the mixture, you should get 4-6 depending how big you make them.
5. Heat the oil and fry in batches of two or three - these should take 10-12 minutes.

Serve with large tomato slices, lettuce and wholemeal burger buns with sweet potato chips.

Chicken Dippers

(Serves 4)

4 chicken thighs boned and diced

100g ground almonds

1 egg beaten

2 tbsp coconut oil

1. Cut the chicken into 2cm strips.
2. Dip the chicken pieces in the egg, then coat them evenly with the ground almonds.
3. Heat the oil in a large pan and fry the chicken pieces, turning them occasionally until they are golden and cooked through.

Meatballs

400g lean minced beef

1 onion finely chopped

1 garlic clove pressed/grated

2 tbsp chopped fresh basil

1 large egg beaten

1 tbsp rapeseed oil

1. In a frying pan heat the oil and garlic on a medium heat.
2. Add the onion and stir fry until soft then remove from the heat.
3. In a bowl add the lean mince, basil and egg, add in the onion and garlic.
4. Mix well together then make into small round balls, this should make 22.
5. You can pop them in the fridge now to use later or add them to the frying pan and fry in batches for 10 minutes, transferring to an oven-dish after frying.
6. Add in a good few dollops of the hidden veg pasta sauce and cook in the oven for 20-30 mins, you can add some grated cheese on top if you want to make a meat ball bake.

Serve with pasta or brown rice. Works particularly well with spaghetti.

Veggie Balls

(Makes about 25 veg balls)

2 potatoes, peeled and grated

1 courgette grated and patted dry

1 carrot grated

2 garlic cloves, grated/crushed

1 egg, beaten

30 g cheese, grated

3 tbsp breadcrumbs

1. Preheat the oven to 200C/180C fan/400F/gas 6.
2. Combine all the ingredients together in a large bowl.
3. Form into small sized balls and place them on a greased baking tray.
4. Bake for 30 minutes and use grill function for the last few minutes until they are a little golden brown on the outside.

Serve with some of the hidden veg pasta sauce and either pasta, rice or mashed potatoes.

Comfort Food

Lamb Tagine (you can use other Meats/Fish or just Vegetables)

500g lean chopped lamb
1 large onion, roughly chopped
2 large carrots, quartered lengthways and cut into chunks
2 garlic cloves, finely chopped
2 tbsp Ras-el-hanout spice mix (found in the herbs and
spice section in supermarkets)
400g can chopped tomatoes
400g can chickpeas, rinsed and drained
200g dried apricots
600ml chicken stock

To serve
Pomegranate seeds
Chopped almonds

1. Heat oven to 180C/160C fan/350F/gas 4.
2. Heat the oil in a casserole and brown the lamb on
   all sides.
3. Remove the lamb and place onto a plate, then add the
   onion and carrots and cook for 2-3 mins until golden.
4. Add the garlic and cook for 1 minute more, then stir in
   the spices and tomatoes, and season.

5. Put the lamb back in with the chickpeas and apricots. Pour over the stock, stir and bring to a simmer.
6. Cover the dish and place in the oven for 1 hr.

When ready, leave it to rest so it's not piping hot, then serve scattered with pomegranate seeds and almonds, with couscous or brown rice alongside.

Lentil and Vegetable Stew

1 cup rinsed red lentils

½ butternut squash

3 carrots

1 sweet potato

1 onion

Low salt veg stock

Tin tomatoes

Squeeze garlic puree

Tsp rapeseed oil

3-4 bay leaves

1. Chop all vegetables.
2. Heat the onion in a hot pan with the garlic.
3. Rinse your lentils.
4. Add all ingredients to the slow cooker and cook for 4-6 hours remove the bay leaves before serving.

Lamb Hot Pot

Pack lean lamb mince

2 potatoes

1 leek

1 swede

3 carrots

¼ butternut squash

1 parsnip

Low salt (or baby stock cubes) - enough to cover

2 tins tomatoes

Squeeze garlic puree

Squeeze tomato puree

1 tsp rapeseed oil

1. Chop all vegetables up fairly small.
2. Heat a pan with the rapeseed oil and purées.
3. Brown the mince in the pan.
4. Add all vegetables into the slow cooker.
5. Add the browned mince.
6. Turn on a low heat.
7. Add the stock and tins of tomatoes to ensure everything is covered.
8. Leave the slow cooker on for about 6-8 hours.

Bean Chilli

1 tin kidney beans
2 tins any other beans (apart from baked beans in sauce)
2 tins chopped tomatoes
1 onion
1 red pepper
1 green pepper
3 cloves garlic
1 red chilli finely chopped (optional depending on whether your family likes heat)
1-2 tsp chilli powder
3 pieces of 80% dark chocolate

I simply add everything (apart from the chocolate) at the same time, and put the slow cooker on for 5-8 hours. Then I add the dark chocolate about 30 mins before turning off and serving.

Spanish Chicken (Quorn)

in slow cooker

Chicken breasts/thighs or Quorn pieces
1 red pepper
1 courgette
1 onion
2 garlic cloves
3 tsp smoked paprika
Squeeze tomato puree
2 tins tinned tomatoes
1 tin chick peas
Juice and zest ½ lemon

Chop vegetables.
I add everything in at the same time and cook for 6-8 hours, stirring occasionally.

Serve with mashed potato and green vegetables, such as broccoli.

Cottage Pie

400g lean minced beef/Quorn mince or rinsed red lentils
Pan of potatoes, peeled chopped and mashed
1 carrot finely chopped
1 swede finely chopped
Cup of peas
Cup of sweetcorn
Cup of grated cheese
Low salt veg stock (enough to cover the mince) or low
salt gravy granules
1 tbsp tomato puree
1 clove garlic pressed/grated
1 tbsp rapeseed oil

1. Heat the oil, garlic and tomato puree and cook the
   mince until brown (do not add lentils if using lentils
   at this point).
2. Add the carrot, swede, peas and sweetcorn with the
   stock (if you are using lentils add them now, you can
   do 50% mince to 50% lentils).
3. Transfer to an oven-proof dish and top with the
   mashed potato and cheese - place in oven at
   190C/170C fan/375F/gas 5, for 30 minutes.

Serve with steamed broccoli or roasted carrots
and parsnips.

Super quick meals

Stir-fry is a great option for a super quick family meal. It is great for children who are happily eating vegetables as stir fry dishes do include a lot of veggies.

If you want a stir fry for picky eaters here are some options to try to get them involved in eating more vegetables willingly:

Butternut squash, carrot and courgette wriggles (simply spiralise these)

Cauliflower or broccoli rice (simply blitz florets down then stir fry for 3 mins in coconut oil)

Home-made sauces to introduce more flavours

Marinade for Meat/Fish/Vegetables/Tofu and Quorn Stir Fry

Juice and zest one lime
red chilli finely chopped (optional)
fresh grated ginger (small chunk)
large splash soy sauce
large splash olive oil

Put all of the above into a bowl together, then mix in your meat/fish quorn or vegetable pieces; leave for as long as possible then transfer from the bowl to the pan and stir fry.

Stir fry Sauce

Juice and zest from one orange
1 tbsp cornflour
2 tbsp hoisin sauce
1 tbsp oyster sauce (you can get veggie versions)
1 tbsp rice vinegar
2 tsp brown sugar

Mix it all together in a small bowl and add to the final stages of the stir fry.
I use whole-wheat noodles or brown rice for extra B vitamins and fibre.

Mexican Scrambled Eggs

2 eggs
½ avocado
4 tomatoes
½ yellow pepper
2 spring onions finely chopped
Tsp smoked paprika
Olive oil

1. Heat the oil in a pan and add all the vegetables.
2. In a separate pan make the scrambled eggs.
3. Add together then add the smoked paprika and avocado before serving.

Serve on whole-wheat or seeded toast.

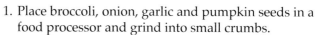

Jazzing up Vegetables

Broccoli Pancakes

6-7 medium broccoli florets
2 tbsp chopped onion
1 small garlic clove, diced roughly
2 tbsp pumpkin seeds
Pinch of pepper
1 egg
3 tbsp plain flour
½ tsp baking powder
Coconut oil for cooking

1. Place broccoli, onion, garlic and pumpkin seeds in a food processor and grind into small crumbs.
2. Add the egg and process again until mixed well.
3. Add baking powder and flour and mix in the processor, scraping the sides.
4. Heat the coconut oil in a large frying pan until really hot and then bring the heat down to medium.
5. Add a tablespoon of mixture and flatten slightly into a round pancake. Repeat until you've filled the frying pan.
6. Cook for 3 minutes on each side, flipping carefully in between.
7. Add a little extra coconut oil when cooking on the second side.
8. Repeat the process with the rest of the mixture.

Maple Roasted Carrots and Parsnips

3-4 carrots

3 parsnips chopped to the same size as the carrots

3cm fresh ginger grated

1 ½ tbsp melted butter

1 tbsp pure maple syrup

1. Preheat the oven to 150C/130C fan/300F/gas 2.
2. Place the carrots and parsnips into the baking dish mixing well with the ginger, butter and maple syrup.
3. Roast for 20 minutes turning occasionally.

Coconut Coleslaw

¼ red cabbage finely sliced

¼ white cabbage finely sliced

1 green apple peeled and grated

1 tbsp shredded or flaked coconut

1 -2 cups full fat natural yogurt

Simply combine all of the ingredients in a large bowl, mix well and serve or keep in the fridge as a side dish.

Shop-bought coleslaw is full of mayonnaise and is unnecessarily fattening. If you don't like coconut simply mix sliced/shredded vegetables with natural yogurt. Play with the flavours - I sometimes add some sultanas for sweetness and a pinch of smoked paprika.

Hidden veg – how to sneak in nutrients

Children and adults should aim to eat a rainbow of naturally colourful fruits and vegetables each day. Each naturally occurring colour group has its own jobs to do in the body, so for optimal health we should eat all colours not just our greens!

Orange – Red, yellow and orange foods are rich in carotenoids. These are powerful antioxidants and help the body to make vitamin A. Carrots, squash, tomatoes, apricots, peppers (anything in this colour family).

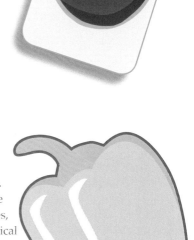

Green – Green foods, particularly dark green leafy veg also contain carotenoids; spinach and kale are particularly good sources. Green veggies are also a great source of calcium especially kale and broccoli. Calcium is very important for developing children.

Purple – foods naturally purple in colour contain a powerful group of antioxidants called anthocyanins. Foods in this group include, berries, beetroot, purple grapes, black beans, kidney beans, plums and prunes, blackcurrants. Antioxidants protect us from free-radical damage.

Consider fruits and vegetables to be antioxidant and phytochemical super-heroes, which help to look after you and enable you to grow bigger, stronger and be able to learn more and do more.

Whilst we all want children to sit and willingly eat vegetables, sometimes there is a need to sneak them in, ideally always offer an actual veg alongside anything hidden so that they do get used to the textures and flavours of individual foods. Don't worry about losing the nutritional value of the vegetables by hiding them, they will still be good for the child even if hidden and blended!

I involve my little boy in making this sauce so he knows what goes in and whilst he would refuse to eat aubergine, mushrooms or spinach on their own he happily eats this sauce!

Hidden Vegetable Pasta Sauce

1 butternut squash
1 aubergine
1 red pepper
1 red onion
2 courgettes
6-8 mushrooms
1 bag spinach fresh or frozen
2 carrots
3 tins tomatoes
Bunch basil
Black pepper
1 tbsp Olive oil/rapeseed oil
2 garlic cloves

1. Chop all vegetables into chunks.
2. Put in a roasting tin with the oil (except the spinach, basil and tomatoes).
3. Grate the garlic (or press) and rub over the vegetables.
4. Roast on a low temperature (150C/130C fan/300F gas 2 for about an hour.
5. Remove roasted vegetables from oven and transfer to the blender.

6. Add the tomatoes, basil, spinach and pepper to
the blender.
7. Blend as much or as little as you need (if very fussy
blend everything to a smooth consistency, otherwise
   leave a few lumps).
8. Transfer to freezer containers, or if using straight away,
   just warm up gently.

You can use this sauce to make a number of pasta dishes:

*Bolognese with lean mince, lentils or Quorn mince (or a
combination of mince and lentils).*

Tuna Pasta Bake.

Just with Pasta and Cheese.

*Lasagne; use the sauce as above,
but layer in sheets of pasta and
cottage cheese before topping with
grated cheese.*

*Chilli; use the sauce as a base, cook
the mince with additional garlic,
onion, red and green peppers and
kidney beans, then mix all together.*

*(If children are particularly fussy about texture,
add in the beans before you blitz).*

This is an ideal base for any number
of dishes, so it's worth making a very
large quantity of it and either freezing
in individual portions or in 'family sized'
portions.

You can also make this in the slow cooker.

Quick ways to sneak in nutrients!

Of course, it's best to get the child to eat food willingly as this helps avoid becoming picky eaters but, as you work on that, here are some good ways to put your mind at rest that they are eating them, whether they know it or not!

Combine vegetables into potatoes when mashing - any root veg works well.

Make hidden vegetable sauces like the above, but with different vegetable combinations.

Add dried/fresh fruit to baking.

Add nutritional boost powders anywhere you can! (e.g. milkshakes, smoothies, porridge).

Make cauliflower rice instead of rice.

Use sweet potato and celeriac in the same way you would use a potato - they both make great chips or roast potatoes!

Soups are a great way to get lots of nutrients into your child, without any recognisable textures or visuals!

If your child won't eat eggs, try poaching an egg and using the yolk to add to their serving of baked beans, this way they get the goodness of the egg yolk (remember all the great things eggs do?!) but without them making a fuss.

Make fresh smoothies and milkshakes; ideally get them

to help, but if you need to sneak in some spinach and you think that will put them off, do that one for them rather than with them! Once in and blitzed spinach is hard to recognise when combined with fruit.

Make drinks fun like watermelon cooler - basically it's watermelon in a glass, but pour it into a fancy glass or small milk bottle.

Swap shop

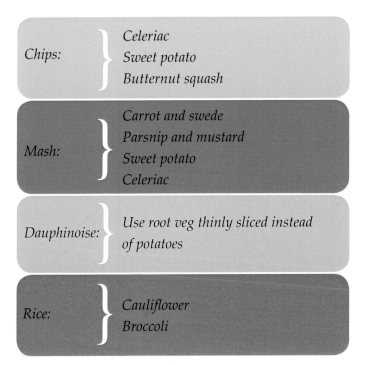

Chips:	}	Celeriac Sweet potato Butternut squash
Mash:	}	Carrot and swede Parsnip and mustard Sweet potato Celeriac
Dauphinoise:	}	Use root veg thinly sliced instead of potatoes
Rice:	}	Cauliflower Broccoli

Every day favourites

Everyone knows that children seem to love baked beans and tomato ketchup, but the shop-bought versions can be full of unnecessary added salt and sugar. These following versions are a cost-effective way to make in batches and freeze, then whenever they want beans or ketchup you can be happy knowing they are also getting the goodness!

Baked Beans

Makes one large saucepan, enough to batch freeze
12-14 individual portions.

1 jar Passata 680g

2 tsp tom puree

2 tsp garlic puree

2 tins haricot beans

½ tsp celery salt

1 tsp ground cumin

½ tsp agave nectar

1 tsp smoked paprika

1 tbsp rapeseed oil

1. Heat the oil on a low heat in a pan (make sure it is one with a lid).
2. Add the tomato and garlic purées.
3. Add the passata, celery salt, cumin and smoked paprika.
4. Drain off the liquid from the haricot beans, rinse then add to the mixture.
5. Increase heat slightly so that the sauce can thicken.
6. Add the agave nectar.
7. Simmer for 30-35 minutes, taste occasionally - you may wish to add more paprika or cumin but try not to add more agave or celery as this will increase the sweetness/salt content.

Tomato Ketchup

Makes one small bottle

300ml Passata
1 tbsp tomato puree
45ml apple cider vinegar
1 tbsp honey
½ tsp celery salt
¼ tsp smoked paprika

Place all the ingredients into a medium sized sauce pan on a medium heat.
Keep on the medium heat for 35-40 minutes, do not let the ketchup stick to the pan, but you need the heat to enable it to thicken.
It will start to bubble, don't turn it down too much but gently stir and keep an eye on it as it thickens – it does take a while but I find it's quite therapeutic to watch!

Whilst children love these everyday favourites cooking them this way is also incredibly good for them. When tomatoes are cooked they become more nutritious, whilst true cooking of tomatoes decreases their vitamin C content, but it increases the levels of lycopene that can be absorbed by the body. Lycopene is part of the carotenoid group (remember the section on eating a rainbow?). Lycopene is a powerful antioxidant and is responsible for the deep red colour in food, in particular tomatoes.

Theme nights

If your child is suffering from food neophobia (basically meaning an aversion to try new foods) then making meal time a fun family experience can be a great non-pressured way to introduce new foods, whilst also being a learning experience about a different culture!

Choose one night a week when you have more time to sit down together as a family, involve the child/children in picking a particular country, this could tie in with a holiday destination, school project or something topical at the time.

Set out your eating area as a 'restaurant'; make it different to how you normally eat, for example you can download free music for any country, use a different table cloth, anything to make it feel like a new and exciting food experience.

Set a challenge to bring the country to life!

Italian Theme

For an Italian theme night this menu encourages self-selection, and this can be a great way to get children to try new things, remember children like to feel in control!

Starter Selection

Bowls of pitted olives
Mozzarella balls with cherry tomatoes halved
Carrot, cucumber and bread sticks with dip

Pea and Mint dip

See recipe on page 62

Main Course

Hidden Vegetable Pasta Sauce, on Fresh Egg Pasta/Dried Whole-Wheat Pasta

Make the pasta sauce as per page 111.
Stir the sauce through your cooked pasta, allow the child to select what they would like to add to their pasta, have 2-3 choices available. (Remember that you are in control regarding what selections you put out, but the child needs/wants to feel in control of their own choices).

Have salad available and ensure that grown-ups are seen to be eating salad and enjoying it! Parental influence is huge; it may take a while, but children who see eating vegetables as a norm will accept them in time. The children may not help themselves to the salad, don't force it on them just enjoy it yourself!

Protein options	*Cooked salmon*
Grated cheese	*Meat balls – see page 96*
Cooked chicken breast	*Veggie balls – see page 97*
Sliced albacore tuna	

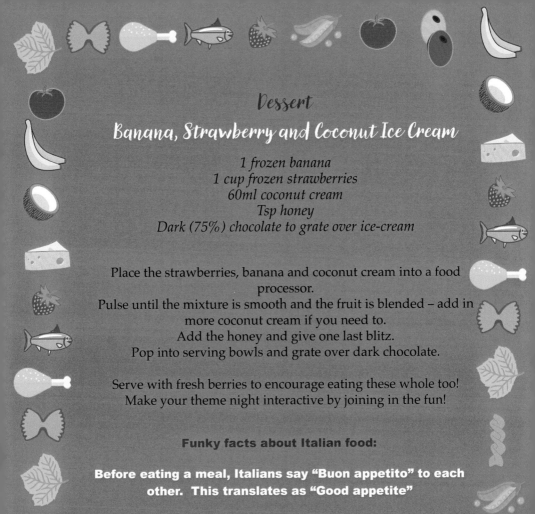

Dessert

Banana, Strawberry and Coconut Ice Cream

1 frozen banana
1 cup frozen strawberries
60ml coconut cream
Tsp honey
Dark (75%) chocolate to grate over ice-cream

Place the strawberries, banana and coconut cream into a food processor.
Pulse until the mixture is smooth and the fruit is blended – add in more coconut cream if you need to.
Add the honey and give one last blitz.
Pop into serving bowls and grate over dark chocolate.

Serve with fresh berries to encourage eating these whole too!
Make your theme night interactive by joining in the fun!

Funky facts about Italian food:

Before eating a meal, Italians say "Buon appetito" to each other. This translates as "Good appetite"

Pasta is the most important food in Italy. Pasta means 'paste' this is because pasta is basically a paste of flour, water and sometimes egg. There are hundreds of types of pasta – how many have you tried?

The Margherita pizza (named after their Queen) was made to showcase the three colours of the Italian flag – Mozzarella (white), tomato (red) and basil (green). What is your favourite pizza?

Can you find out two more Italian food facts?

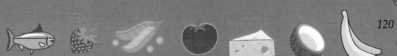

120

Mexican Theme

For a Mexican theme night a menu like this encourages free choice, which can be a great way to get children to try new things; remember children like to feel in control!

Starter Selection

Bowls of tortilla chips
Carrot, cucumber and pepper sticks with Salsa and Guacamole
(this is not the full version of guacamole but encourages children to eat avocado)

Guacamole Dip

See recipe Page 64

Home-made Salsa

4 ripe tomatoes finely chopped, 8 sprigs coriander finely chopped
¼ onion finely chopped, Green chilli (optional),
Juice and zest of a lime

Simply mix all together

Home-made Spicy Tortilla Crisps

2 tbsp oil, 1 tbsp Cajun spice mix, 8 plain tortillas

Heat oven to 180C/160C fan/350F/gas 4.
Mix the oil with the Cajun spice mix. Brush the spiced oil over tortillas, stacking the tortillas on top of each other as you go.
Cut the stack into 8 wedges.
Separate the wedges and evenly spread out on baking sheets and bake for 6-7 mins until golden and crisp.

Main course
Wraps/Tacos

Children love to make their own so ensure there is a
selection of options available.

Bean chilli – see page 101
Chilli with hidden veg sauce see page 111
Roast/slow cooked chicken, pulled apart
Vegetables – i.e. peppers, onions, mushrooms to make fajitas
If you know they will eat sweetcorn add a bowl to the table,
it may not 'go' but if it is a vegetable they will gladly eat,
then it should be available!
Grated cheese (half and half with grated carrot, if you use Red
Leicester cheese they probably won't even notice the carrot!).

Dessert
Avocado 'Chocolate' Mousse

Although not technically a Mexican dessert, it uses
avocado so it can join in!

1 banana
1 avocado
1 tbsp raw cacao powder
Squeeze of date nectar/Maple Syrup

Simply combine all ingredients in a processor, transfer to
individual dishes and pop in the fridge.
Chill for at least 2 hours before serving.
Use more banana to sweeten rather than more date nectar /
Maple Syrup.

Make your theme night interactive by joining in the fun!

Asian Theme

For an Asian theme night, a menu like this encourages free choice, which can be a great way to get children to try new things; remember children like to feel in control!

Starter Selection

Chicken dippers - see page 95
Satay sauce - see page 86
Ribbons of colourful vegetables
Prawn crackers

Main Course

Thai Curry

see page 89

Salmon Fish Cakes

see page 83

but add in a small amount of red Thai curry paste to the mix

Homemade Egg-fried Rice

Cook the rice according to the packet instructions.
Make scrambled eggs with the 3 eggs and add to
the cooked rice.
Stir in the frozen peas to the cooked rice and
egg mixture.
Add a splash of soy sauce.

Dessert

Mango and Coconut Ice cream

*2 frozen bananas (always peel prior to freezing,
and place in a freezer bag)
Small cup frozen mango
1 carton coconut cream*

Place the frozen mango, banana and coconut cream
into a food processor.
Pulse until the fruit has combined and looks
smooth (may take a while and you may need to add
more coconut cream).
Serve straight away as the frozen fruit will
start to melt!

**Make your theme night interactive by
joining in the fun!**

Puddings and Cakes

Children clearly love puddings and sweet treats but as explained in the section about how the brain expects reward, try to keep food rewards to a minimum and puddings as a treat.

If you need a few every day options for something to finish a meal off rather than have a traditional pudding, try one of the following;

Natural Yogurt with Fruit and Honey

Yogurts for children can be full of all sorts of added sugar, sweeteners and colours. Yogurt is important for children for the fats, calcium and protein, and if it is live yogurt this is also good for their gut health. Added sugar can undo a lot of this good so whenever possible try to make your own, it's easy and you can control the flavours you have.

Here are some flavours you can try, all you need is a few spoons of either full fat natural or thick Greek yogurt and your chosen fruit, a hand blender or food processor.

Blueberry and honey
Strawberry and banana
Mango and coconut

Fruit itself can also be a good post-meal option. Remember when serving grapes to cut them in half length ways (never width ways).

Dried fruit is a good option but always check that the fruit has not been coated in sugar (manufacturers sometimes do this!).

Here are some 'proper' pudding recipes:

Fruity Crumble

Non-cooking apples, I use Braeburn or Pink Lady
Ripe pears
1-2 tsp Cinnamon
Small cup coconut sugar
Large cup plain porridge oats
Drizzle maple syrup
Thick Greek yogurt

1. Chop fruit.
2. Place in bowl add cinnamon and maple syrup.
3. Place in a pan with a little covering of water.
4. Simmer on a very low heat (to be honest I forgot about mine but think it was on about 1hr 10).
5. Place fruit in bottom of an oven dish.
6. Mix oats and coconut sugar in a bowl then cover the fruit.
7. Place in oven for about 40 mins at 180C/160 Fan/ 350F/Gas 4.

Instead of serving with custard, serve with a large dollop of Greek yogurt.

Mango and Coconut Ice cream

2 frozen bananas (always peel prior to freezing, and place in a freezer bag)
Small cup frozen mango
1 carton coconut cream

1. Place the frozen mango, banana and coconut cream into a food processor.
2. Pulse until the fruit has combined and looks smooth (may take a while and you may need to add more coconut cream).
3. Serve straight away as the frozen fruit will start to melt!

Banana and Choc Chip Ice cream

2 frozen bananas (always peel prior to freezing, and place in a freezer bag)
1 carton coconut cream
1 small cup cacao nibs

1. Place the frozen banana and coconut cream into a food processor.
2. Pulse until the fruit has combined and looks smooth (may take a while and you may need to add more coconut cream).
3. Once you have the mix to the desired consistency add the cacao nibs and stir in rather than use the processor.
4. Serve straight away as the frozen fruit will start to melt!

Nutty Berry Cheesecake

Selection of nuts to make the 'biscuit' base. You can use any combination of nuts, but I would try to include walnuts for the essential fatty acids.

Base:
2-3 cups mixed nuts
4-5 tbsp melted butter
Topping:
2-3 tbsp mascarpone cheese
2-3 tbsp thick Greek yogurt
2-3 tsp lemon curd
Cup of berries - blueberries work well, but so do strawberries and raspberries or any combination

1. Using a food processor blend the nuts into a crumby slightly paste looking consistency.
2. Add the melted butter.
3. Transfer to individual glass ramekins patting the base into the dish and making a flat surface and bake in the oven for 10 minutes on a low heat (170C (150 fan) /325F/gas 3).
4. Allow the bases to cool.
5. In the food processor mix the berries, mascarpone, Greek yogurt and lemon curd then spoon onto the base in the ramekins.

Banana Chocolate Cheesecake

Selection of nuts to make the 'biscuit' base. You can use any combination of nuts, but I would try to include walnuts for the essential fatty acids.

Base:

2-3 cups mixed nuts

1 tsp raw cacao powder

4-5 tbsp melted butter

Topping:

2-3 tbsp mascarpone cheese

2-3 tbsp thick Greek yogurt

3-4 pieces 70% cocoa dark chocolate grated

(keep some to one side for serving)

1-2 bananas

1 banana sliced to serve

1. Using a food processor blend the nuts and raw cacao powder into a crumby slightly paste looking consistency.
2. Add the melted butter.
3. Transfer to individual glass ramekins patting the base into the dish and making a flat surface and bake in the oven for 10 minutes on a low heat (170C (150 fan)/325F/gas 3).
4. Allow the bases to cool.
5. In the food processor mix the bananas, mascarpone, Greek yogurt and grated chocolate then spoon onto the base in the ramekins.
6. Add sliced banana on to each and a sprinkling of grated dark chocolate.

Oaty Muffins

Smaller quantities make 6 muffins, larger makes 12)

2-4 eggs

2-4 bananas

1-2 tsp baking powder

1-2 cups oats

Use this as your base then you can add any of the following or your own flavour combinations

Raisins

Fresh/frozen blueberries

Dried apple and cinnamon with raisins

Crushed walnuts

1. In a bowl mash the banana.
2. Add the eggs, oats and baking powder and mix well.
3. Add any flavour combination.
4. Spoon into muffin tray.
5. Bake for 20 minutes at 180C/160 fan/350F/Gas 4

As an extra boost of nutrients, you can add in some nutritional powders such as Acai Berry, spirulina, wheatgrass, flaxseeds or chia seeds.

Banana Nut Muffins

4 bananas, mashed with a fork (the more-ripe, the better)

4 eggs

1/2 cup almond butter

2 tbsp coconut oil, melted

1 tsp vanilla

1/2 cup coconut flour

2 tsp cinnamon

1/2 tsp nutmeg

1 tsp baking powder

1 tsp baking soda

1. Preheat oven to 180C (160 fan)/350F/gas 4.
2. In a large bowl, add bananas, eggs, almond butter, coconut oil, and vanilla. Using a hand blender, blend to combine.
3. Add in the coconut flour, cinnamon, nutmeg, baking powder, baking soda.
4. Blend into the wet mixture, scraping down the sides with a spatula.
5. Distribute the batter evenly into the lined muffin tins, filling each about two-thirds of the way full.
6. Bake for 20-25 minutes, until a toothpick comes out clean.
7. Serve warm or store in the refrigerator in a re-sealable bag/tub.

Brownies

1 cup almond butter

1/3 cup maple syrup

1 egg

1 avocado

1 tsp vanilla

1/3 cup cacao powder

1/2 tsp baking soda

1. Preheat the oven to 160C (140 fan)/320F/gas 3.
2. In a large bowl, whisk together the almond butter, syrup, egg, butter, and vanilla. Stir in the cocoa powder and baking soda.
3. Pour the batter into a 9-inch baking pan.
4. Bake for 20-23 minutes, until the brownie is done, but still soft in the middle.

Choc Seedy Fridge Squares

1 cup cashew nuts

½ cup sunflower seeds

½ cup unsweetened desiccated coconut

½ cup chia seeds

60ml maple syrup

1 tbsp vanilla

2 squares 70% dark chocolate – broken up as small as
you can

4 squares 70% dark chocolate to melt

1. Place the cashew nuts, sunflower seeds, coconut and chia seeds into a food processor and blitz.
2. Add the vanilla, maple and chocolate pieces, and blitz again.
3. Line a shallow baking dish with baking paper and put the mixture in.
4. Place a bowl over a small pan and gently melt the remaining dark chocolate.
5. Drizzle the dark chocolate over the mixture, spreading it out to the corners.
6. Place in the fridge and chill for at least 2 hours before trying to cut into neat squares.

The "Bake Well Tart" Addition

I didn't want to write a cookbook for children without including some more traditional cakes and biscuits (healthy versions of course!), however, those who know me well, will know I am not a baker!

My approach to cooking is to combine things together and hope for the best, and, as I find out each time I attempt to bake, this approach doesn't work well with baking! You may have noticed that none of my 'cake' recipes involve flour!

I have enlisted the help of my friend and professional baker Kate Jordin from The Bake Well Tart to provide me with some actual baking recipes with measurements and everything! Kate is an award-winning baker who prides herself on her creativity and using top quality ingredients. Whilst I am

a big anti-sugar crusader for unnecessary and excess sugar I am not one to shy away from a good quality home-made cake once in a while and Kate is who I would turn to, to make it!

Kate Jordin from The Bake Well Tart

Guilt- free Carrot Cake
(sugar-free, gluten-free & dairy-free)

Cake:
100ml sunflower oil
4 medium eggs
3 tbsp date syrup
150g gluten free self raising flour
100g ground almonds
1 tsp cinnamon
1 tsp mixed spice
1 tsp bicarbonate of soda
100g raisins
300g grated carrots
¼ tsp xanthan gum

Topping:
250g dairy free/free from cream cheese
2 tsp date syrup

1. Grease and line an 8" cake tin and preheat the oven to 180C/160C fan/GM 4.

2. Using a free-standing mixer, or the old fashioned whisk and bowl method for an extra work out, beat together the oil and date syrup, then add eggs one at a time.

3. Sift together the flour, cinnamon, mixed spice, xanthan gum and bicarbonate of soda, stir in the ground almonds and add to the oil, date syrup & egg mixture.

4. Add the raisins and carrots, give the mix a good stir, then tip into the cake tin and bake in the oven for 45 minutes - 1 hour or until a cake tester comes out clean.

For the topping - when the cake has cooled, whisk the syrup into the cream cheese then spread lovingly over the top of the cake.

Sticky Banoffee Loaf

80ml sunflower oil
7 tbsp honey
2 medium eggs
2 large bananas mashed
65ml milk
1 tsp vanilla essence
225g wholemeal self raising flour
1 tsp bicarbonate of soda
1 tsp cinnamon
100g chopped medjool dates

1. Grease and line a 9" cake tin and preheat the oven to 165C/145C fan/GM 4.

2. Using a free-standing mixer, or the old fashioned whisk and bowl method for an extra work out, beat together the oil and honey, then add eggs one at a time.

3. Mix in the mashed bananas and vanilla essence.

4. Sift together the flour, bicarbonate of soda and cinnamon. Alternate adding to the wet mix with the milk until it is all combined. Stir in the dates.

5. Bake for 1 hour or until a cake tester comes out clean.

Oaty Apple Biscuits

100g butter
3 tbsp honey
125g wholemeal plain flour
50g oats
½ tsp cinnamon
50g dried apple rings, chopped up into small pieces

1. Grease and line a baking tray and preheat the oven to 180C / 160C fan / GM 4.

2. Using a free-standing mixer, or the old fashioned whisk and bowl method for an extra work out, beat together the butter and honey until it is very creamy.

3. Sift the flour, add the oats, cinnamon and chopped apple and stir into the wet mix.

4. Spoon balls of biscuit mix onto the baking tray and bake for 10-15 minutes or until golden brown.

Drinks & hydration

In terms of keeping hydrated, children can be pretty bad at remembering to drink - especially when they are at school. Did you know that boys are 76% more likely to be dehydrated than girls?[1]

1. The Health Sciences Academy – Dehydration at School and reduced brain function

1. The Health Sciences Academy - Dehydration at School and reduced brain function

Being dehydrated (even a little bit) can lead to headaches, irritability, poorer physical performance and impaired cognitive and emotional function in children.[1]

What's the best thing to drink? Plain water. Plain water is essential for brain function. Yet for children of secondary school age, soft drinks containing sugar currently make up 29% of their daily sugar intake. We have already seen in the introduction to this book that sugar has a detrimental effect on concentration and intellectual development, yet still many drinks aimed at children are high in sugar.

Plain water is the best and cheapest option, but sometimes we do need something more exciting, here are some options to try:

Banana Berry Milkshake

1 banana
1 cup any mixed berries fresh or frozen
300ml almond milk (unsweetened)

Simply whizz all up together.

Chocolate Banana Milkshake

1 banana
1 tsp raw cacao powder
300ml almond/hazelnut milk

Simply whizz all up together.

Hot Chocolate

300ml hazelnut milk
2 tsp raw cacao powder
1 tsp maple syrup

1. Heat the milk slowly in a pan.
2. Add in the cacao stirring and whisking on a medium heat.
3. Drizzle in the maple syrup just before removing from the heat.

Tropical Fruit Smoothie

½ cup spinach
1 apple chopped
2 slices fresh or frozen pineapple
½ cup frozen mango
200ml coconut water

Use a mixer/juicer/bullet to whizz all together.

Watermelon Cooler

¼ watermelon

Hand blend or add to mixer and serve straight away.

Fizzy drink alternatives

Mango and Raspberry

300ml sparkling water chilled
½ ripe mango
Cup fresh raspberries

1. Chop the mango and blitz the mango and raspberries with a blender until they resemble a fruit puree.
2. Put the fruit puree in the bottom of a tall glass and top up with the sparkling water.

Pineapple, Ginger and Lime

200ml sparkling water chilled
100ml fresh pineapple juice
Fresh ginger grated
Squeeze of lime juice

Add all the ingredients together and give it a quick blitz.

Blackberry and Honey

300ml sparkling water chilled
½ cup fresh/frozen blackberries
Drizzle of honey

1. Blitz the blackberries then add the honey and place in the bottom of a tall glass.
2. Top up with the chilled sparkling water.

Snacking

Given the chance, children would snack all day long! I know from my own personal experience with my little boy, and I will often find him rummaging in my bag or packing himself some snacks to take with us, as if off on a great expedition, even on the shortest of outings! As with adults snacking can be quite good for keeping blood sugar levels stable, as long as we are snacking on the right foods!

There are, thankfully, now quite a lot of healthier snack foods particularly aimed at the younger (pre-school) children, but unfortunately there are still a lot of inappropriate options available too. Snacking on high sugar/salt/fat options will create unstable blood sugar levels, and can also alter behavioural patterns, as the sugar kicks in and then again as it drops. It can also stop the child from wanting to eat at meal times.

When out and about I do always make sure I have a selection of emergency snacks with me, to avoid having to opt for an unhealthy option if the child is saying they are "starving", in the way that only children can when they have only eaten an hour earlier!

Try not to always have just sweet snacks even if they are healthy sweet options, as this still encourages a sweeter tooth to develop. These are some handy snack options I always use:

Breadsticks

Carrot, cucumber sticks

Cubes of cheddar

Dips – see recipes in the lunch section

Raisins

Nuts, dark choc chips and jumbo raisins (careful with very young children and nuts)

Dried fruit bars

Fresh fruit

Always have plain water with you in a BPA free container, as unfortunately many venues only offer unsuitable drinks options for children.

Thank you

From the start of this book to it's completion has only been a time-span of approximately three months. This is fairly typical of the way I work once I set my mind on something! However, in working on something so time consuming and detailed in such a short space of time, there are lots of favours to be called in and lots of professionals to do the bits I cannot do myself.

Firstly, the food elements, in making this book I have had to cook a lot of food! So, thank you to my little boy Owen for being chief taster from a child's perspective, and to my husband Darren for helping to come up with some of the ideas and of course, then eating them. Anyone who visited our house during the making of the book was encouraged to sample anything and everything!

Thanks also to my ever-patient parents who have been involved in editing, eating, taking photos for the food blogs and babysitting so that I can study / write / cook.

For the official copywriting elements thank you to Louisa Sando-Patel of Bright Owl Copywriting and to everyone who has read the book and added comments and edits, thank you for the input and feedback!

To make the book look lovely and fit with the ideas in my head! Thank you to Mikki Longley of Mikki Longley Creative, there has been a lot of illustrations and design work in my short time scale!

For business support from day one, thank you to Barbara Hodgson of the Women in Business Network (WIBN) thank you for the ideas and support over the last six years.

I have to say a special thank you to Marc Ford, business coach for giving me a bit of a kick to follow my dream of aiming to improve nutrition for children in any small way that I can.

Thank you also to Rachel Hargrave of RDZ PR for helping me to tell people about this book!

Thank you to Sarah at Goldcrest Books and to Claire at Full Square for publishing and printing and making all of the other elements come to life as a real book!

To my family, clients, everyone I network with and to those who are in my Facebook group and have followed the journey of this book, thank you for the continued support, encouragement and feedback, and I hope you enjoy the book.

Last but by no means least, thank you to my husband Darren, who did say that 'normal' people would take many months even years to plan and budget this kind of project, but that wouldn't be me! Thank you for putting up with the chaos, the endless reading, cooking, eating! Thank you for supporting me and enabling me to follow my dream.

Reference sources

It's fair to say that I personally find the subject of nutrition fascinating! I have studied extensively in this subject over the years, and nutrition continues to be both controversial and contradictory. When putting together this book I was inspired by recently completing a Health Science Academy course on the *"Impact of Nutrition on the developing brain"*. I also reviewed historic and current scientific papers, journals and publications to see what is happening on a global scale to address some of the current medical conditions that have been attributed to lifestyle changes in the past 40-50 years.

We can see that there are more health concerns around weight and obesity than ever before and the evidence suggests that the problems can begin in childhood. This seems an obvious place to start addressing their nutritional intake as a form of preventative health. The majority if not all of the studies and work being carried out agrees that there is far too much sugar being consumed, but the health impact of all this sugar is only just being felt. As discussed it isn't all to do with weight. Hopefully in years to come some big changes around the manufacturing of food for children (and adults) will take place, thus looking at nutrition not just calories as appears to be the case currently.

There are many people researching and working behind the scenes to improve nutrition. Unfortunately, not all of this research is seen as headlines, and initiatives often overly focus on one area and not the whole picture. I have tried to condense and simplify from all of these reference sources, and my own extensive studies over the years, and I hope that you will find this book helpful and useful in enabling you to take control and gain understanding of the food you and your children eat!

INTRO

Tackling Obesity through the healthy child programme - A framework for Action NHS/University of Leeds

Public Health England - *Sugar Reduction - the evidence for action*

Scandinavian Journal of Medicine and science in sports 143 - 149 - *"Physical activity as a preventative measure for coronary heart disease in early childhood"*

The Journal of Clinical Endocrinology and Metabolism; *Childhood Obesity* Volume 89 issue 9

Department of Health - *Healthy Child Programme - the first 5 years*

World Health Organisation - *Sugars - intake for adults and children*

Public Health England - *Health Matters: Child dental health 2017*

NUTRIENTS TABLE

Health Sciences Academy - course materials for Advanced Child and Brain Nutrition Advisor

Dr Mercola - speaking at the Restorative Medical Conference on Iodine and Child IQ

Vitamin D and Depression: Where is all the Sunshine? US National Library of Medicine - National Institutes of Health

Medical News Today February 18 - *What is Serotonin and what does it do?*

Health, Exercise, *Nutrition for the very young* (HENRY) - Gov.UK

The Soil Association's *'Out to Lunch'* campaign - Gov.UK

GENERAL

Obese babies and young children: an approach to paediatric management - Mary CJ Rudolf Consultant Paediatrician and Professor of Child Health at the University of Leeds and Leeds PCT, Leeds General Infirmary, Leeds, UK

The Obesity Code - Jason Fung

Health Sciences Academy -
How food changes your DNA - effect of nutrition on your epigenome

Building a human brain - Neuroscience 101

Probiotics: natures antibiotics - Human microbiome and probiotics

Science Report - *how are your brain and gut connected?*

Can diet affect a child's academic achievement? - adverse dietary influences on academic success

NHS - *Diabetes: cases and costs predicted to rise*

Nutrition reviews - *Associations between nutrition and behaviour in 5-year old children* V 44 issue 3

Science Daily - Vanderbilt University Medical Centre - *Molecular link between diabetes and schizophrenia connects food and mood*

Are dietary patterns in childhood associated with IQ at 8 years of age? A population-based cohort study - Dr Kate Northstone, Department of Social Medicine, University of Bristol

House of commons Library - *Food Advertising on Television May 2012* (the 2004 Public Health White Paper- choosing health; making healthy choices easier

Fast food consumption and academic growth in late childhood (Purtell and Gershoff 2015)

Epigenetics - feeding the obesity and diabetes epidemic? Institute of Experimental Genetics at Helmholtz Zentrum München (Neuherberg, Germany)

Epigenetics - being overweight adds distinct epigenetic marks to DNA

Epigenetics - could turn on obesity switch

Examining a Developmental Approach to Childhood Obesity: the Foetal and Early Childhood Years, institute of medicine 2015

British Heart Foundation - *Policy statement - Trans fats*

Department of Health - *Technical guidance on nutrition labelling -* March 2017

Faculty of public health - *food poverty and health*

Global nutrition report 2016

World Health Organisation - *Sugars intake for adults and children –* Geneva WHO 2015

Index